Human Time Bomb

HUMAN TIME BOMB:

THE VIOLENCE WITHIN OUR NATURE

C.A.A. Savastano

Campania Partners, LLC

Acknowledgements

I am thankful to my wife, family, friends, supporters, and my publisher for providing advice and encouragement during my endeavor to write a second book.

FOR MY GRANDFATHERS

Editorial Reviews:

"An impressive tour de force. Savastano shows a mastery of relevant work in such diverse fields as biology, anthropology, and the history of intelligence. He creatively combines insights from this scholarship and addresses fundamental questions about the human condition and the prospects for overcoming our propensity for violence. Each chapter will challenge readers to rethink old assumptions."
- David T. Beito, Department of History, University of Alabama, Author of T.R.M. Howard: Doctor, Entrepreneur, and Civil Rights Pioneer and From Mutual Aid to the Welfare State

"This is a work is a slap in the back of the head, a wake-up call, and a serious reality check as to the true human condition. It should be read by every individual, but especially by policy makers at all levels of government. Entire communities of serious researchers in the fields of ethno-biology, psychology, cultural anthropology, and military history have documented these issues – only to have their conclusions ignored because they are too unpalatable to the general public, and out of favor with political agendas in all quarters. Our species is unique, both in its abilities, and its evolutionary heritage. Whether it can survive that uniqueness remains to be seen, unless it can confront its true nature that appears increasingly unlikely."
- Larry Hancock, Historian and Author of Shadow Warfare, Nexus, and Creating Chaos

"Savastano blends his knowledge of political and military history into a psychological examination of our propensity for aggression. What I most appreciated was that "Human Time Bomb" offers a lens into modern social issues (such as reparations) and an evolving culture based on social media where social barbarity is often disguised as well-intentioned advocacy. It is a long, hard look into the potency of our collective shadow that is extremely relevant in today's socio-political climate."

- R. Blackstock Psy.D., LP, CAADC

"After reading this book, you will no longer ask why is this happening (regarding human violence), where it comes from as well as why we are facing it..."

- Dr. Richard Burke, Medical Health Professional

TABLE OF CONTENTS

CHAPTER 1:

DOMINATION, AGGRESSION, AND VIOLENCE

"You will become as small as your controlling desire; as great as your dominant aspiration"

- James Allen, Author

Despite popular claims of some people being intrinsically merciful, this premise disregards the fact that any human also can be relentlessly cruel. Each of us can be morally dominant leaders with a natural capacity for protective behavior or potential tyrannical killers bent on senseless brutality. Certain biological triggers under the proper circumstance incite or frighten even the most passive individual into violent deeds because aggression has always been with us in various forms. The genesis of this latent need to dominate others and our surrounding habitat ceaselessly spurs debate among experts. While the victim, perpetrator, and location of violence are important facts to specific cases, the deepest motivational question is what lurks within the human condition that allows us to justify such means? Some may claim it is merely a threat assessment or criminal advantage crafted in the higher mind, and while this might explain some later complex planning, the origins of violence rest deeper in the human brain. This challenges us to consider what parts of the brain truly enacts dominance, aggression, or violence and do we even command our biology or does it in some manner dictate the choices to us?

Violence is unacceptable in any but defensive circumstances to many humans but justified dominance is a stabilizing influence. Biology and environment create a need for every animal to dominate others at times and establish themselves in a functional hierarchy. Democratic elections are a form of domination achieved by the consent of the individuals voting, they give their collective will to a single person to represent them in a government. Because an elected official should have the most desirable skill set and leadership qualities, they are elevated in the dominant political hierarchy. Unfortunately, this same recurring dominance urge can, under different circumstances; illicit violent tyrannical repression.

Our murderous tendencies were (according to a study written in 2014) the cause of nearly 1.5 million deaths across the world per year.[i] Humanity's aggressive urge is an enduring animalistic tendency of the deeper brain and environmental factors such as population increases can present new and often-competing interests that may initiate such urges. Why does our asserted evolutionary superiority fail to prevent this lethal desire in the most rational of people? Some answers lay deep within the circuitry of our brains limited by the design of control systems and the overall chemical balance. Disturbance in any part of this delicate arrangement unleashes our most brutal impulses without a quick natural inhibition or concern for the resulting damage. Experts attribute this failure to a portion of the brain that predicts social cues and what expectations of reward and punishment our behavior may induce. Mental illness, cultural biases, drug use, and environmental factors all increase stress and this disrupts our natural ability to limit violence. Several experts question is this aggression and violence a natural part of our evolutionary biology or is it a product of our environment?

The Influences of Nature

Those embracing the concept of nature being a solely benevolent force in human existence have written poetry, literature, and music to praise its humbling majesty. Our desire to embrace nature has repeatedly inspired human attempts to use a more natural means for nearly every activity but most still maintain artificial luxuries. Some humans eschew modern conveniences or add extremely complex methods to achieve less manufactured results because of the reported therapeutic and health benefits. Indeed, nature can be an introspective force that can teach us valuable lessons but there is another side to nature residing within mammalian biology.

A psychological study composed in 2016 listed more than one-thousand species of mammal to determine the most vicious killers targeting their own species, and humans were at the top of the list. Dr. R. Douglas Fields offers "Step back and view our species objectively from the outside, the way a zoologist would carefully observe any other animal...The brutal reality could not be more evident or more horrifying." An endless barrage of lethal daily violence reported in our constant news cycle supports the disturbing propensity for humans to destroy other people. "We are the most relentless yet oblivious killer on Earth. Our violence operates far outside the bounds of any other species. Human beings kill anything. Slaughter is a defining behavior of our species. We kill all other creatures, and we kill our own... Carnivores kill for food; we kill our family members, our children, our parents, our spouses, our brothers and sisters, our cousins and in-laws. We kill strangers. We kill people who are different from us, in appearance, beliefs, race, and social status. We kill ourselves...We kill for advantage and for revenge...We kill friends, rivals, coworkers, and classmates. The reasons can be traced back to our primate ancestors, which are exceptionally violent creatures...the reasons for this rampant self-killing appear to relate to our big brains and conscious awareness... fierce territoriality and living in social groups."[ii] The one common factor is human beings kill those who threaten their beliefs, social status, relationships, politics, and territory whether a genuine threat exists or not.

Several contextual questions offered by Stanford University neuroendocrinologist Robert Sapolsky may reveal motivations deeper than often acknowledged by society. What occurred in the brain of someone being violent minutes before they acted? What occurred in the hours, days, and months previous that led to these circumstances? Are there instances from their distant past influencing these recent events that include analyzing even the structure of their behavior in contrast to evolutionary development? Several factors require assessment for a more comprehensive understanding of why violence seems our eternal companion. "Both dominance and aggression are animalistic traits, handed down to humans through a succession of predecessors as a means of survival." These notable elements can "...play a significant role in defining human personality."[iii] While social dominance and aggression are part of verified human inclinations, some experts suspect violence is an adaptive strategy to assure the perpetrator's evolutionary success.

"We are evolutionarily and genetically predisposed to snap in deadly violence...The problem is that our neural circuits...cause us to explode in rage...deep in the brain beneath the cerebral cortex where consciousness arises." While some believe murder and violence are just culturally influenced traits, every human can possess a "genetic component with high heritability" for heightened levels of aggression.[iv] Family studies and those utilizing identical twins support that impulsive aggression and irritability, which differs from premeditated aggression, is transmissible to future generations. Thus, our biology can establish the propensity for greater violence and some naturally present abnormalities can further expand later aggressive characteristics.

The possibility of mental illness plays a foundational role in the propensity for cruel behaviors and psychological disturbance that further enhances aggression includes but is not limited to "borderline and antisocial personality disorders". Though disorders alone do not always lead to violence, when they do the outcome of these behaviors can include spousal abuse, job loss, assault, rape, and murder. Among violent offenders, forty-seven percent of men and twenty one-percent of women reportedly have antisocial personality disorder. These issues further inspire an overdeveloped impulse for verbal and physical aggression in some humans that suffer related mental problems. This is just a portion of the larger issue and one academic report offers that classifying "violence narrowly from the perspective of psychological dysfunction shirks the larger truth that the biological roots of rage exist in all of us. The leading risk of death throughout the prime of life is not disease. It is violence."[v]

According to 2014 United States Center for Disease Control statistics, homicide was the fifth largest cause of death in all age brackets from one year to forty-four years of age. One related scientist offers a random "...unconnected insane assailant is less probable to kill us than someone we are quite familiar with, and suicide is the second most frequent killer of people between ten and thirty-four years old. The most important factor in violence is not pathology, psychology, or politics--it is biology." At least forty percent of mammals use lethal violence and this number according to research was likely an underestimate.[vi] The analysis of related data suggests an increased urge for violence can be inherited and suggest overly aggressive cultures might affect such tendencies in humans. "Humans emerged from a very long lineage of species-great apes and before them primates- that all expressed relatively high levels of lethal violence...When you immerse an animal in a particular environment, it evolves genetic-based strategies for dealing with that environment. There is good reason to believe this reflects a real genetic or innate tendency to solve problems with violence."[vii]

We can usually determine a potential for violence by relevant biological factors, among the important distinguishing factors are hormonal differences in males and females. Unfortunately, some people attempt to claim there are no differences between males and females despite substantial evidence. Such ideas are flawed and do not accurately present the reality of human existence because there are several vital similarities and differences selected by the mammalian evolutionary path. These verifiable differing traits promoted our survival and every individual is a unique mixture of them. Even studies of identical twins' support that no two people are exactly alike in form and temperament because of differing mental and physical qualities in the most physically similar examples of humanity. Individuals might appear similar on the surface but still have obvious and subtle physical differences that uniformed generalizations do not consider.

Psychologist Dr. Steven Pinker has addressed the attempt of some modern researchers to redefine the facts regarding biological science in the service of claiming that humans are a blank slate until extensive socialization occurs. Pinker suggests critics of sociobiology "have sought to base the political ideas of equal rights and equal opportunity on a false biological premise: that all human minds are equal because they are equally blank, equally free of innate, genetically shaped abilities and behaviors." "The politics and the science must be disentangled...Equal rights and equal opportunities are moral principles, he says, not empirical hypotheses about human nature, and they do not require a biological justification, especially not a false one."[viii] Most verifiable testing from several different spheres of science would support Pinker's reasonable criticism of the modern tendency to confuse politics with science likely fueled by confirmation bias.

Human genetics is limited to the expression of biological traits that evolution has selected to benefit our species and ensure our survival. Centuries of scientific data and study established there are two sexes, male and female based on the fact that every human being ever present on Earth and that shall be present born naturally was formed by a male sperm and female egg. Sexes are not social constructs but factual representations of the natural world supported by refined and proven science that all claims to the contrary lack. There are prominent physical differences in males and females based on skeletal, muscular, weight, and hormonal variations.

Researcher Hannah Holmes notes, "The human female is on average, a few inches shorter than the male. This is a telling detail. Often, a sharp size difference between sexes indicates a violent relationship between males. The goal of a male gorilla, for instance, is to wage war against all other males to control a group of females. The losers don't get to breed. As a result of their high-stakes mating system, male gorillas have evolved to nearly twice the size of females." Chimpanzee's that have "looser groups" and humans that sometimes practice monogamy have even greater reductions in size variation based on gender. This reveals that normal socialization can have biological effects that can benefit or affect males but, in some cases, environment causes stark reversals.

Male animals are generally the larger in most cases but "occasionally" the female can become larger, such as female spotted hyena's who some experts believe hormonal changes for survival generated increased testosterone and thus more dominant behavior and physical traits emerged. Within insect species this reversed dimorphism extends to "grotesque extremes", due to size differences females might even confuse tiny males with prey. At least one spider type will strum the web of a larger female to identify themselves as more than just food and one aquatic creature is so minute in comparison to the female he just latches onto her body in any random location. "He latches on with such conviction that his head more or less dissolves and he becomes a sperm generating tumor with fins". Even more pathetic is a type of deep-sea male worm that does little but generate sperm "his entire life deep in the female's gut."[ix] There are substantial examples of biological differences in the sexes of every species including humans. Yet human desires eternally seeking dominance can render damage to the environment that does not frequently occur in the natural world.

Professors at the University of Victoria reportedly "described humans as 'superpredators' who don't follow the typical rules of other carnivores in the animal kingdom--which can have devastating consequences for wildlife populations."[x] Thus, our biology can establish the propensity for greater violence and some other naturally present abnormalities can further expand later aggressive characteristics. While the average large predators (wolves and lions) often select young, injured, or sick animals for prey, humans act oppositely and select the healthiest and largest targets. This can have a negative impact environmentally by removing the best animal specimens from the local gene pool and inadvertently damaging the environment's future health. The largest targets increase the physical risks to the hunter based on size but human males seek them out and if one is not present males intentionally enter dangerous environments to seek animals more easily procured locally. If males are committed to their survival, why do they seek out prey or resources that are more dangerously gathered? Males overcome all these dangers to earn group status.

Primitive males formed groups to provide social interaction, a hierarchy, improve hunting skills, and establish status to present themselves as suitable mates for eligible women in the related society. Women too formed hierarchies by creating gatherer groups, converting prey animals into food and clothing, raising children, and seeking group status. This division of labor shared between sexes was not the oppressive social construct some lackluster modern philosophers contend, but more likely, a utilitarian assignment of duties tailored to assure the survival of the species. Observable divided labor trends in the animal kingdom suggest that mating pairs form a reciprocal labor system to survive.

The emerging cooperation between two unrelated animals poses dangers to each participant in the form of exploitation by negative interactions. Positive examples of such activity create a "reciprocal altruism" where "each individual pays a cost...for another's gain but achieves an even greater benefit...when its actions are reciprocated" to "keep costs of cooperating and benefits of cheating low." Such behaviors in the animal world occur within hermaphroditic fish that trade egg parcels and take turns performing each gender role with various mating partners. "Other mechanisms such as partner choice and partner fidelity lend stability to reciprocity strategies like egg trading by lowering the costs and risks of investment in cooperative partnerships."[xi]

Humans engage in cooperation through biologically influenced parental investment behaviors that include females nurturing children, males hunting or gathering to sustain the family, and both sexes naturally protect their home and offspring from predators. Evolutionary anthropologists' debate if biology or social adaption furthered already present natural gender differences into forms of parental investment such as maternal nurturing and paternal "dominance striving". Organisms ranging from germs to primates with female and male counterparts reveal

9

versions of this process by fulfilling roles to further parental investment based on their natural development.

This is not to say normal variations will not occur from other influences but the vast majority of examples adhere to these established patterns in nature. One academic study would be shocked "not to find associations of basic parental investment or male-male competition with biological factors, such as sex hormones, given the established role of these factors in nonhuman sex differences". "Feminine psychological adaptations for parental care have been linked to the psychometric construct of empathy, and reduced empathy in men has been linked to lower thresholds for aggression...."[xii] These roles were not developed from any mere social construct but rely on biological determinations.

Evolution designed the male role based on strength, aggression, dominance drive, and the social need to compete with other men or the environment by acquiring territory. Females are more empathetic, nurturing, and represent the only humans able to produce offspring and to assure the survival of humanity. A pregnant or nursing mother cannot reasonably hope to protect themselves and offspring while being forced to gather and hunt and this places an overriding biological importance on the life of women that does not extend to men and children. The natural evolution of this system would place men in the environment hunting and most women and children in a safer location not by some ancient oppression but more likely for survival. The majority of unrecorded human history began prior to any modern concept of gender oppression and those seeking to employ such arguments ignore significant biological and historical evidence.

Human societies without any strong nurturing female influences are easily prone to violence and destructive tendencies from their naturally aggressive inclinations leading to destabilization. Those with insufficient dominant males face consistent oppression, lack organization, and heap the usual division of labor assumed by men for millennia on the back of women. Similarity of task does not equate to fairness and the current propensity of some groups desiring the sexes to be identical is not based on verifiable science or overwhelming evidence. They fail to recognize that reversing the current natural hierarchy forces each sex into a contrary role against natural human aptitudes and consequently reduces the success rates of all related endeavors. Among the largest biological difference between the sexes is a higher propensity for violence in males and this suits them for environmental competition. The survival of our species requires the protection of women from environmental dangers and thus humans formed roles to accomplish this end. While verifiable oppression can and does occur, the formation of biologically influenced hierarchy roles guards against the extinction of humanity.

Biological influences play a significant part in developing the human capacity for violence and evidence offers testosterone can, but does not always; influence the probability of aggressive responses to external factors. A US National Institutes of Health study offers testosterone "manifests itself in various intensities and forms from; thoughts, anger, verbal aggressiveness, competition, dominance behavior, to physical violence. Testosterone plays a significant role...in aggression and on the development of the muscular system that enables their realization." Differing testosterone levels in males and females presents certain gradual biological advantages and consequences. Abundant testosterone does offer greater muscle development, less fat on average, stronger bone density, sperm production, improved concentration, sexual desire, and hormonal advantages. Simultaneously an overabundance can promote acne, liver disease, weight gain, insomnia, headaches, prostate cancer, aggression, and rapid mood changes.

"This type of mechanism appears to explain sex differences in anatomy and some aspects of sex differences in behavior. For example, testosterone present during a particular period of fetal development in mammals induced the development of the male reproductive tract and genitalia. If androgen levels are low, as is normally the case in females, this development does not occur...A similar control for male aggression has been demonstrated in a number of laboratory animal species."[xiii] Biological studies explain that female mice injected with testosterone a single time at birth respond far more sensitively to biological aggression than counterparts who developed naturally and this carried into studies that included human females that were accidentally exposed to increased levels of steroids prior to birth. The same verifiable result too occurred in women possessing greater than normal "testosterone concentrations" or who injected testosterone at some point in their life. The human body for the vast majority of people naturally balances its hormonal levels over time and tampering with this system can lead to permanent unintended consequences. To deny the role of biological differences influencing later behavior requires someone to abandon the scientific facts.

"Attempts have been made to deny or minimize the role of genes in human behavior, but the evidence for their role is overwhelming. We share 98% of our genes with the chimpanzee, our closest relative, thus our behavior cannot be divorced from that of other species. Even our capacity for language, which mediates the transmission of culture, depends on brain structures that develop via genes." "About half of individual variance in personality traits is due to genetic differences and half to environmental ones". "In short, all human behavior is mediated by the brain, which develops through the influence of genes that are the products of natural selection." [xiv]

Biology is a vital element contributing to a propensity for violence but alone does not render genetic dispositions into actual behavior. Using positive influences, counseling, and trust building social experiences can mitigate negative biological potential. Violent behavior requires strong influences to activate destructive tendencies, biology must set the proper stage and environment provides the proverbial actors. How the human drama proceeds vary on the specific related elements but neither biology nor environment appears to control the overall effects alone. Together a genetic propensity for violence with the proper environment can initiate catastrophic results.

The Influences of Environment

Every human seeks to dominate their environment, everyone they encounter, and everything around them to varying degrees. Two general classifications of social domination often seen in most human interactions are "...sociable dominance and aggressive dominance"[xv]. A sociable dominant person seeks to be the center of activity; they too have better relationships, and receive positive attention because they do not engage in violent or threatening activity. This form of dominance is consistently more productive to the overall system by incorporating a basic need in the process of human evolution into social rewards. A society can channel this need into a reciprocal system where most have the opportunity to express their talents, voice concerns, and have the chance but not assurance to become dominant using mutually beneficial social interactions.

Oppositely, if a person lacks the desire, understanding, or intent to engage others productively they use aggressive dominance. Such personalities will threaten, shout down, shame, and cajole others causing them to receive desired attention but it is negative attention and can destabilize their relationships. Negatively perceived aggressive domination often isolates and

13

further inspires additional poor results because the aggressor may not understand why their natural desire to be dominant repeatedly fails or its oppressive success creates a backlash. People using both the sociable and aggressive dominance methods can be successful and each group has similar biological traits but a combination of factors decides why they engage in differing forms of dominance.

Sexual development produces striking aggressive and empathetic differences in the human dominance strategy to achieve success. Variances between human sexes appear to expand at the age of three when environmental forces reinforce biological factors according to studies noting gender differences in dozens of societies. Young girls spend more time cooperatively working and boys competitively play more, older girls have greater exposure to infants and develop empathy often absent in older boys. Aging males spend less time at home socializing with their mother than females and groups of children will naturally self-segregate by sex and age as multiple factors create starkly different gender traits.[xvi]

These growing differences in the sexes provide complimentary skill sets in future parents and functional social arrangements that promote species propagation. Among the many benefits complimentary parenting offers is a nurturing mother's ability to offset antisocial behavior. Supportive mothers provide benefits to fathers and offspring by curbing male aggression, promoting the free expression of feelings, and nurturing the development of ethics. A strong maternal figure helps children build self-esteem, develop empathy, improve cognitive development, and promotes mental health. Long-term female social influences seemingly provoke enduring biological changes in males with several studies identifying "possible suppressive effects of romantic relationships, marriage, or fatherhood on testosterone levels in men". Women

14

are one of two key influences in the promotion of healthy relationships and stable children.

An involved father will improve a child's cognitive ability, language development, social competence, and the development of successful coping strategies. His presence reduces instances of hyperactivity, teen violence, delinquency, and evidence does suggest a strong paternal figure aids in the development of less sex-stereotyped beliefs. A stable paternal influence can offset "maternal depression", "economic hardship", and compliments female influences by normally engaging in a beneficial collaboration to expand human society.[xvii] Unfortunately, not all parents have strong levels of parental investment and some act in opposition to assuring stable family relationships.

Abusive or absent parents can drastically increase the chances of mental illness, aggression, and violence in their offspring. While many of the difficulties experienced by children in divorced families do fade over time and may result in more stable parental arrangements, some effects persistently linger. A New Zealand study cites during the first two years following a divorce both parents and children normally experience physical and emotional problems. By four years into the social adjustment process, many girls prove more resilient because they can recover as early as primary school based on their age and the divorce timeline. Boys with only a female parent contrarily "exhibited behavior problems for as long as six years."[xviii] Divorce according to multiple verifiable studies has "negative consequences for the mental health of some offspring that persisted into adulthood." Divorce was associated in a minority of people with moderate increases in mental deterioration and serious mental illness but seems with most people to impact normal public conduct, educational attainment, and quality of life.

The children of divorced parents have a higher rate of being divorced themselves and significant detrimental changes may occur by the disruption of naturally forming social relationships over time. While in a minority of cases some children do experience benefits from divorce, this is largely from the removal of abusive or anti-social parents from the home. It appears trauma during formative periods can occur just by the absence of a parent and be worsened by the loss of both or if the child is subjected to abuse. However, most parents are loving and extremely protective due to biological and social investments that occur during the course of a child's life.

Two parents increase mental development and health in children by securing a stable environment with multiple parental influences and this provides an extra person to assume portions of the labor a single parent would bear alone. Based on prior studies it seems feasible that all supportive couples with varying levels of hormones have a greater positive impact raising children than single parents will, because they provide two parents with separate but complimentary biological and social traits. This does not suggest that single parent households do not benefit drastically from both parents' involvement; they do, but data infers two parent households possess better success rates.

While some well-intentioned parents might believe shielding children from the stress of developing adult responsibilities is the proper course, those lacking regular social development do pay consequences. Among the consequences is a lack of emotional maturity because some parents do not instill many socialization or coping abilities in their children. The cost of not educating children on the necessary skills for maturity according to multiple scientific studies has created a modern extension of adolescence. Adulthood based on some expert analysis may now surpass the legal age of eighteen and extend to twenty-five, and this persistent immaturity has serious prices. The United States Centers for

Disease Control and Prevention queried "over eight million 13- to 19-year-olds" that comprised several racial, economic, and regional backgrounds. They asked participants how they spent time outside of school and tracked these activities over extended periods and the results are troubling due to the stark regression in prior standards of maturity based on age.

"Beyond just a drop in alcohol use and sexual activity, the study authors found that since around 2000, teens have become considerably less likely to drive, have an after-school job and date...Perhaps their socializing and more salacious interests have simply gone digital via texting, sexting, and online pornography." "By the early 2010s, it also appeared that 12th graders were going out far less frequently than 8th graders did in the 1990s." "What's more, the decline in adult activity was consistent across all population, and not influenced by race, gender or location." San Diego State Professor Jean Twenge notes that people that are biologically 18 years old now act 15 and that modern teenagers are not more virtuous but lazier or prefer childish pursuits to the development of adult responsibilities. The pattern of slowing development appears centered around children with greater economic stability and children in lower income families still have to accept earlier responsibility and develop adult oriented skills faster due to necessity.[xix] This exemplifies some differing factors in development are driven by necessity and better education or financial advantages do not promote maturity without commensurate responsibility. Additional stress or challenges and the lack of constant help can drive some people to excel beyond all normal expectations.

The very environment a creature resides in proves to be a constant source of stress from predators, starvation, weather, disease, pests, and resource competition. This and several other considerations push animals toward possessing a controlled safe area in which to shelter and reside. Territoriality is an overwhelming survival instinct that animals possess to mark areas of their influence without verbal communication that humans inherited from our forbearers. This instinctual desire to secure a home and prime territory with limited available resources forces competition and often violence in animals and humans.

People require a safe and clean territory for decent standards of living because such an environment reduces stress levels, promotes concentration, and contributes to overall well-being. Reportedly, these benefits can extend to increased rates of healing from sickness by just observing prime natural territory and tested medical patients fared better in recovery when they viewed a natural landscape as opposed to those with only construction or stone around them. Such ideas would support an intrinsic beneficial connection between humans and our natural environment that defies our modern path towards a more artificial existence. Inversely, an undesirable territory often features regular aggression, violence, and fuels likely depression from a lack of accessible preferred environments.

A lack of access to resources and natural environments does not just negatively influence humans but affects the natural world as well. "Male birds who can't win an attractive territory" usually do not reproduce "while females flock to landed gentry." Some female birds choose to be one of multiple mates to a single male of great territory rather than a single mate of someone with bad territory. "Although playing second fiddle will lower her odds of producing a healthy family, so will settling for a second-rate territory." The cost of failing to secure any territory can lead to some members of a species experiencing permanent negative consequences. "Male great horned owls who fail to stake a claim spend their entire lives sneaking from one territory to the next, poaching prey. They are locked out of the mating cycle entirely. These homeless "floaters" are also the first to go hungry when the (prey) population dives, and presumably they're the first to die of starvation."

This behavior is not limited to just birds, as other species behavior would match such mating success based on the possession of territory. Aging male lions ejected from their pride's territory await starvation without any support group for hunting or protection. Coyotes abandon sick and old members that become too much of a burden and force them from pack territory. Mating fish will defend territorial areas and large groups of fish have been observed to defend the best feeding areas from outside incursion by lone invaders. "An even worse end looms before a homeless water boatmen insect: He's eaten by his competitors."[xx] While animal territorial conflicts are usually limited to necessity, they are often violent and no mercy is shown to opposing creatures.

We repeatedly can observe every organism's desire for expansion and the deep fear of not achieving biological success inspires tremendous acts of violence but the necessary violence for survival practiced by early humans transformed in most instances to violence for domination. With the rise of armies, nations, and defined cultural boundaries aggression regularly occurs for ideological, political, and military reasons and not in defense of rational policy. Several influential people rely upon the lower brain's tendency to keep the public unreasonably afraid of contrary or competing interests to serve their own. Failing to conceive or care about the eventual harms, many seek to wield primal instinct like a weapon to serve whichever variant cause they might represent.

Fear is one of the brains most primal influences and according to one scientific paper just "a single traumatic experience can initiate a cascade of dynamic brain processes which may result in enhanced vulnerability to subsequent stressors or even in a break-down of normal functioning as seen in the pathologies of the trauma spectrum."[xxi] A brain under regular environmental conditions is not laden with stress and memories form with autobiographical or "cold" memory. This type of memory "contains knowledge about life-time periods and specific events" and these events are usually associated with declarative "hot" sensory and emotional memories of the environment (sounds, smells, and visual flashes of the scenery). "However, in traumatized persons, sensory and emotional memories are activated by environmental stimuli" and these traumas manifest without cold memory attachments and autobiographical context forming a "fear network". A related study proposes that activation of a single fear memory might cause a whole network of memories and bad feelings to activate such a network of fears. This reportedly increases connections between the existing network and can even add new more debilitating ideas and triggers to the existing network of traumatic stress. "However, contrary to expectations, it seems that emotionally arousing stimuli, not necessarily related to the traumatic event, suffice to activate the whole fear network."[xxii] Such an emotionally based network can alter the different standard controls in the mind for violent reactions that defy normal brain function.

Whether desired or not, evolutionary design in the lower brain uses fear to activate our evolutionary responses and we instinctually prepare to face danger or attack perceived threats. In the average brain, the amygdala performs correctly by flashing a warning as our prefrontal cortex is still assessing the actual threat. This portion of the lower brain is able to register a threat before we are consciously aware but it is not concerned with precisely gauging a threat. While the higher brain seeks to contextualize what it perceives the amygdala seeks to neutralize possible threats and such imprecise targeting can make us lash out without knowing if a true danger exists. A brain lacking the ability to control the amygdala's signals can suffer permanently distorted emotional responses without logical connections to the original trauma. Substantial trauma essentially can alter the functionality and even structure of the brain to a varying extent.

Environmental influences curb the overuse of violence utilizing psychological responses to victims that extend to the natural world and possible reprisal prevents many types of animals from killing each other without vital need. Most successful animals compete for dominance in a group but do not murder the large majority of their competitors due to possible rage reactions of the victim and those associated with them. "Animals tend to stay within the rules because the rules are enforced by the victim. In fact, fights are relatively rare once the animals work out their dominance hierarchy." However, subordinate animals naturally still attempt to disrupt the established hierarchy to increase their standing, remove an opponent, and may endanger the entire group structure. Although fear may cause a person to flee rather than oppose a threat, another primal motivator in humans can activate deep confrontational responses.

Disgust is the powerful mechanism that fuels some aggression created by the insular cortex of the human brain. It causes the protective biological and emotional responses we experience after tasting rotten food, breathing a foul smell, or seeing a violent death. "It's in our everyday life. It determined our hygiene behaviors. It determines how close we get to people. It determines who we're going to kiss, who we're going to mate with, who we're going to sit next to. It determines the people we shun, and that is something we do a lot of." Early observable incitement of the disgust mechanism might cause "Kids in the playground to accuse other kids of having cooties. And it works, and people feel the shame when disgust is turned on them."[xxiii] Because mere threats of reprisal do not prevent violations of these unspoken instinctual rules when "a dominant animal continues to attack a defeated animal that has submitted", a typical disgust influenced response to this action is for others to attack the creature breaking the rules. The proverbial law of the jungle evokes physical "retaliation" by the incited group and such enduring rules even appear in human culture proscribing attacks upon those rendered defenseless.

An important evolution in the disgust mechanism is the expansion of it to include moral disgust, but this subjective feeling can vary based on each individual's definition of acceptable behavior. Anyone that considers something disgusting regularly finds such things immoral as well and most populations consider animalistic qualities disgusting; this aversion extends to public exhibition of nudity, sex, death, and filthy substances. Nevertheless, disgust reactions extend beyond physical stimulus and can guide social interactions, outside forces (individuals, groups, corporations, nations) seeking to manipulate human reactions can alter the concept of what many consider socially acceptable despite the facts.

Increasingly differing perceptions of repeated subjects can inspire the disgust reaction to create an insidious cycle of perceived moral outrage leading to immediate actions without full understanding of any context. Moral outrage is a treacherous arena because the brain's insular cortex is fallible and subject to error without deeper considerations and supports visceral feelings of being correct despite contending evidence. Such flawed interactions occur when a person or group cannot justify its unreasonable demands and opt instead of debate to demonize opposing people. Among the probable reasons this occurs is because it allows a more attractive target for releasing this instinctual aggressive reaction. To resist the disgust mechanism requires rational considerations that are not emotionally satisfying but eminently more productive.

When irrational disgust regarding people of different backgrounds, politics, and religions occur, they can result in aggression and violence. The possible root of such feelings may emerge in part from our human predisposition to consider unknown influences negative to current social hierarchies. Mistrust of unfamiliar cultures has long triggered a defensive suspicion in people because we have evolved to mistrust unknown influences. Similar primordial disgust associated with the smell and sight of dead humans proved so influential that some cultures even proscribed touching anything dead and relegating those professionals dealing with the dead to the lowest ranks in a society. Ancient cultures had no concept of modern science but they explained natural aversion with fables of the dead being evil rather than being a source of disease. While primal disgust can guide us to unreasonable and abhorrent behavior, it too has protected many from dangers once beyond our rational conception.

Yet accurately distinguishing between acceptable and unacceptable proves challenging when normal behavior triggers disgust in those who misread repetitive biological cues as being moral judgments. A substance in our brain called dopamine influences sections related to pleasure and reward and it significantly increases when our emotions guide us to punish others. This can become an endless cycle of unjustified behavior hijacking the brain's design to reward itself based on perceived "moral" actions. Compound that cycle with social influences and societal politics and this quickly can lead to daily outrage determined by a mounting irrational bias that feeds the reward desire.

Separating biological signals from justified action plays a role in the ever-shifting social constructs of modern society because another region of the brain that registers facial recognition and empathetic response too has a strange reaction when those of other cultural backgrounds are considered. When people observe someone experiencing distress that is unlike them, their natural response to feel concern is reduced and this applies to most humans tested of different cultures. It would suggest that all bias against dissimilar people is not merely a social issue but has some biological influences and further understanding of the related influences might allow us to retain a natural skepticism of new influences but dismiss unjustified impulses.

Genuine or perceived offenses can trigger the same aggression or violence in response to violations of what a person considers socially acceptable. "Subjects report that they would be angered by being passed up by a bus driver, but only if the driver is supposed to stop there. Thus, frustration by itself...does not consistently anger us, but being wronged does." This connection between transgression and aggression is supported by observing that actions which "restore equity" (viable excuses, apologies, payment of damages, or retribution by a third party) and reduce anger related to the violation. Even taking no action or the conscious avoidance of seeking retribution can succeed but the study reveals the only seeming way to reduce anger with certainty is attacking the transgressor in some way to create a more equitable result.

Remarkably, it does not matter if a person is unjustified; the mere perception of feeling as if they were a victim induces hostility without rational justification. Weighing each occurrence on a case-by-case basis can stop perceived aggression from overwhelming a society. Thriving cultures must insist on rational disagreements to facilitate a mutually beneficial existence predicated on contextual facts and be careful to distinguish between true injustice and the aggressive human tendency to lash out when anything makes us fearful or disgusted. This is our very biology whispering that needless violent behavior and unfounded judgments pose a threat to our existence and the success of our collective survival. Unfortunately, humanity in many cases expanded the original use of retaliation to dominate possible competitors and this aggression targets not just legitimate threats but perceived ones as well. Yet doing so prevents any chance for mutually beneficial alliances, consumes resources, and leads to escalating permanent counterviolence. Fear and disgust present unmistakable biological challenges feeding our desires for aggression because our biology relies upon them in times of distress.

Other Forms of Dominance and Aggression

Overt violence is not the only expression of dominance desire and aggression, one aforementioned study in addition reveals that dominance competition does not require violence and has vital benefits. Human societies contribute to the limitation of overt and uncontrolled violent aggression by channeling this desire to benefit those seeking to express it more productively with competition. The modern inclination in some countries to remove reasonable competition from education and sports and seek to reward all participants might lead the expression of dominance via means that are more destructive. We should not confuse attempts to shield children from harm with beneficial adversity such as high educational standards, behavioral ethics, and normal means of competition to harness useful dominance and aggression.

Some in modern society believe the prevention of most normal pressure and social challenges is required for a healthy child. They do not consider the biological need for adversity, responsibility, and natural desire for earned rewards and this misplaced sympathy denies children defensive skills necessary for adult life. Thus, seeking to modify a critical social outlet that has existed for most of history will likely have some long-term negative effects by suppressing a natural desire for genuine competition and earned rewards that can lead to violence and crime. If we fail to harness the competitive desire naturally present in humans, it likely will negatively express itself via other means.

Competitive athletic sports provide humans team-building skills, socialization, leadership roles, greater confidence, and assist developing coping abilities. There must be a temporary victor and defeated to establish a consequence to our actions, if a person or team does not strive to improve it suffers under normal circumstances and will seek to correct this deficiency. While a loss may be temporarily upsetting to defeated teams, it will give them coping skills required for meaningful losses in the future. Failing to develop basic coping skills in a controlled environment forces a person to learn in uncontrolled situations with greater consequences. The path to possible victory can inspire vital resilience a person or team would never realize without using constructive outlets for competition. These interactions can further teach young people to face necessary pressure and overcome the challenges presented.

A related study reminds us "The ability to perform under pressure is necessary to achieve goals in various domains of life...'Pressure is defined as presence of situational incentives for optimal, maximal, or superior performance.'...These processes enable an individual to regulate physiological and psychological states to help movement and decision-making that help goal achievement. Individuals who are unable to employ effective coping skills...affected by pressure may underperform, relative to their skill level." Every person will have significant moments in his or her life hinging on quick decision making under extreme pressure and must be able to cope with it. "Coping strategies that help an individual regulate perceived demands in an important moment could enhance an individual's ability to attend, concentrate, and perform effectively under pressure." This can allow people to defy pressure or excel facing such adversity and potentially increases their coping and performance abilities that may extend to defying stress as well.[xxiv]To lessen the negative influences of aggression we must channel it to useful dominant behaviors with beneficial results.

Professional sports and international physical competitions represent a huge worldwide financial market that generates benefits and entertainment to billions of people because of its obvious roots in our natural tribal desire for asserting dominance. Such huge public events can inspire a pseudo-religious devotion because physically brutal displays allow us to express aggression based on emotionally shared crowd experiences. Some related data even suggests humans can express neurological processes that normally fuel criminal aggression with productive competition. The presence of the right environmental conditions can transform aggression into productive expressions of dominance but sometimes almost no amount of mental fortitude might prevent dark thoughts.

While generally aggression has a clear trigger based on reasonable threats or danger, even the most innocent sources can propel our minds toward violent imaginings. Cute aggression is the human response to an overload of positive emotions; people according to psychologists have flashes of aggression and violence to counteract overwhelming feelings of adoration. This does not mean we actually desire to harm the subject but such thoughts "appear to be an involuntary response" the brain initiates to regulate emotion.[xxv] A study of the phenomenon linked cuter animals with emotional thought centers and the cuter a subject was the more activity generated. It appears negative thoughts counteract extreme feelings of endearment that can be dangerous to rational perspectives and what some might call abnormal thoughts prove to be natural defenses in the proper instance. Violent thoughts have been within us since the first primitive developments of the human condition as both means to dominate and internal defense mechanism. Nevertheless, our brains are not just subject to internal manipulation but minute external threats that influence rising aggression in some environments.

Diseases and parasites represent another environmental consideration beyond our internal genetic predispositions toward violence. The toxoplasmosis parasite is a common organism found in feline excrement and some biological research links this creature to increased aggression. Those diagnosed with Intermittent Explosive Disorder (IED), a condition featuring sudden hostile overreactions to minor stimulus, "were twice as likely to have been infected by the toxoplasmosis parasite compared with healthy individuals with no psychiatric diagnosis." While IED does have the genetic component for heritability without the parasitic influence, an increasing amount of evidence suggests this infection changes "people's brain chemistry to cause long-term behavior problems. Previous studies have linked toxoplasmosis to schizophrenia, bipolar disorder, impulsivity and suicidal behavior."[xxvi] Our usually beneficial associations with several domesticated species might also expand our negative proclivity for aggression.

Yet it takes little more than proper circumstances to illicit rapid mental changes in the most rational of people and where might the path lead if such a person was confronting a target of aggression they can easily dominate? Dr. Robert Sapolsky discussed such a hypothesis when conjecturing on his response to capturing Adolph Hitler. Despite being an intellectual and law-abiding person, he possessed several reasons to desire Hitler's suffering and circumstance might allow him to veer widely from the paths of acceptable behavior. During his speech, his first inclination is to arrest Hitler and turn him over to the proper authorities, then he further comments on what desires came to mind when he considered how to treat the Nazi war criminal.

"What would I do if I had Hitler? And if I let myself go there it wasn't hard to think about it. Sever his spine at the neck, take out his eyes, puncture his eardrums, cut out his tongue...I had this fantasy at various points as a kid and sometimes I still do. And when I do my heart beats faster and my breathing gets faster."[xxvii] This highly intelligent expert feels the exact same aggression and rage far less calm and stable people would under the proper circumstances. Anyone can think and be violently aggressive and no external diabolic force moves our hands but rather biological influences can overpower those unaware of how to curb them. A senseless killer within us eagerly responds to fear and disgust impulses and repeatedly succumbing to these base impulses changes our brains.

CHAPTER 2:

ANTI-SOCIAL CREATURES

"When someone is anonymous, it opens the door to all kinds of antisocial behavior, as seen by the Ku Klux Klan.""

- Philip Zimbardo, Psychologist

Several environmental factors have augmented our means to dominate but perhaps no other influence has so quickly changed humans as technology because technological innovation and unregulated access to weapons can disrupt the ability of societies to mitigate lethal expressions of dominance. Often trivial reasons inspire violence in high crime, low income, and heavily populated areas because our naturally territorial instincts are poised closer to the surface. Increased population promotes greater competition and what seems unthinkable in more forgiving environments occurs daily in other places. Such data suggests adverse environmental factors appear to accelerate the development and usage of lethal dominance and no definitive single biological or social factor renders a person violent but multiple negative factors working in unison do.

A major restructuring in human socialization occurred with the rise of online culture, the introduction of online business, and social media platforms. In 1998 one study that later was supported by several examples indicated that Internet use affected social relationships and community participation. The cost of greater online activity translated into less real-life experiences and direct socialization with family and friends. The creation of social media has drastically increased the amount of time younger people spend watching a screen and this drastically reduced "communication both in the family and in the wider social environment". Another scientific paper reports, "...the past 10 years, the rapid development of social networking sites...has caused profound changes in the way people communicate and interact". Although social networks enable an individual to interact with a large number of people, these interactions are shallow and cannot adequately replace everyday face-to face communication."

Online communication does have benefits; it allows communication, promotion, analytics, information gathering, and business opportunities. Social media provides the ability to contact a distant person, conduct outreach (artistic, charity, and support pages), help in an emergency, and offers entertainment to various different segments of the population as well. This medium can begin possible useful relationships but alone does not establish or maintain them, this is only possible with voice applications or phone calls, using cameras, and several interactions that include personal conversations but require a range of direct social interactions. No online interaction is a complete substitute for personal human relationships because all humans require frequent social interaction with live people for their mental health.

The consequences of social media overuse and obsession are several because the process exacerbates potential or existing feelings of depression and loneliness leading to increasing stress and psychological issues. It provides the ability for someone to detach from social human contact and slide into largely just online contact. Additionally, "...some researchers have associated online social networking with several psychiatric disorders, including depressive symptoms, anxiety, and low self-esteem...With the development of social networks, the time children and adolescents spend in front of the computer has significantly increased." A 2019 World Health Organization report states explicitly that infants should not be exposed to electronic screens because of the likely detrimental effects.[xxviii] One study during 2014 reported a statistically positive correlation between time spent on social media and depressive symptoms.[xxix]

Mistaken online perceptions and information can easily sway users and potentially influence depressive symptoms based on false indicators. The chance for a mistaken impression or miscommunication increases the more emotional and visceral a subject and can lead to escalating arguments, personal attacks, and even threats of violence due to the digital environment seeming to present no direct consequences. Consider how many destroyed careers or personal lives have resulted from a comment made on social media that offended even an anonymous detractor. Years of study, work, and success can vanish due to a single comment; one forever memorialized for others to audit that feeds their disgust mechanism and fuels outrage.

One media report stated that online "comments 'are extraordinarily aggressive', without resolving anything...psychologists say this addictive form of vitriolic back and forth should be avoided-or simply censored by online media outlets-because it actually damages society and mental health." This applies to all such irrational behavior despite its origins but the chance that special interest groups will abandon donations and the digital bully pulpit to improve community mental health remains improbable. Yet there are eventual costs to unchecked aggression or antisocial behavior for extended periods. Largely overlooked by many are the supported associations between depression and violence which some "...findings suggest an association between violent behavior and depression or depressive symptoms in many different disorders."

"A Swedish study compared the criminal records of 47,158 depressed individuals with the records of 898, 454 people with no history of depression matched by age and sex. Those in the depressed group were approximately 3 times more likely than the general population to commit violent crimes, such as homicide, attempted homicide, aggravated assault, or robbery." "Extensive literature exists on the relationship between depressive symptoms and violent behavior in general cohorts of children and adolescents...The association between violence and depressive symptoms is particularly common in children with conduct disorder." This study is notable because of its group size and Nordic countries make excellent general testing groups due to largely similar biological and social backgrounds without significant variable external cultural influences.

Scientists analyzing depressive associations found observable indicators that could predict future violent behavior in some children. "Besides being sad, depressed people often feel disgruntled, resentful, or irritable. Such emotions can lead to violence in people who are predisposed to such behavior, especially when confronted with severe frustration...Patients are more likely to have increased depressive severity, poorer impulse control, and a history of substance abuse. The presence of a substance abuse disorder and poor impulse control renders violence more likely." "Anger has been associated with both depression and violence. This association is more often present in males and children or adolescents. Depressed males are less likely to experience clear depressive feelings or to be aware of these feelings; instead, they present with increased irritability or anger, which can result in violence."[xxx]

Scientific review underpins the fact that depressed children display greater problems controlling their rage and this can intensify existing problems and transform depression to impulsive violence against themselves and others. Another institutional review tested groups of depressive violent patients with severe mental disorders. The group with a greater amount of baseline depression was consistently more violent in every test group compared with patients suffering from less depressive symptoms. While the connections between depression and violence are not all yet demonstrated it appears that childhood trauma, abuse, and drug use are important factors in related cases. What are the alternatives and can we disengage people in the grip of spiraling depression augmented by largely online social interactions?

Reporter Christina Farr offered her experience of detoxifying from social media to observe the results after removing these applications from her phone. Tracking systems provided by social media companies measuring a user's time online ironically caused the change in her behavior. Trying to give up a photo-sharing platform reminded the reporter of withdrawal symptoms akin to purging caffeine and she noticed empty feelings and unconsciously seeking the deleted button on her browser for another prior deleted social media application. The experience reminded her of a conversation with a former Google project manager who commented on applications that were habit forming. He also ominously stated that social media was "hijacking our minds" and the reporter later states it occurred to her after weeks of abstaining from social media her normal usage was "anything but intentional".

It became clear when normally using social media the reporter would feel that nothing important was going on if she had nothing interesting to post. "I felt a growing urgency to start planning something big or make a change to stay relevant. Without social media, that pressure melted away. I started to enjoy life's more mundane moments and take stock of what I have today". When the reporter consulted modern research on the issue, she found studies constructed to limit social media usage and this resulted in the significant decline of depressive symptoms.[xxxi] Experts have warned us the effect of social media on human brains will take decades of more comprehensive investigation to comprehend the full effects.[xxxii] We have not just created technology without knowing its long-term effects but have now plunged ourselves into this psychological morass of the unknown.

Another looming specter in the social media conversation is growing censorship; this act increases aggression and further incites greater negative behavior by isolating those voices with dissenting opinions.[xxxiii] It often condemns minor infractions with the exact severity of major ones and thus conflates normal impulsive mistakes with genuine destructive behavior. The forced absence of discussion or debate on issues of controversy with inconsistent standards of unbiased enforcement adds to existing user disenfranchisement. While obvious violations of legal speech should be enforced for the public good and do exist, increasingly biased public and official groups have abandoned context to embrace a culture of ceaseless punishment often based upon little evidence without neutral considerations. Conversely, the allowance of destructive antisocial behavior founded upon subjective ideas far exceeds the practice of unfair censorship.

Some people from all backgrounds and politics have embraced constant expressions of digital aggression that have detrimental effects upon them and those engaged. Several tactics include ruining the lives of people deemed to have violated the group doctrine and this is observable from the litany of celebrities and public figures destroyed in dozens of such cases. Even those among the attackers would fall victim to such practices of unchecked aggression, a former online activist explains prior having a lucrative job and many friends who all shared the same political and social beliefs until he challenged someone in the group. The digital mob he supported for years eventually targeted him and this confrontation allegedly motivated the group to discredit and renounce him publicly. These actions cost him many friends, his job, and he now uses a pseudonym in public fearing the mob could return to finish what they started.

When the former advocate's transgression was declared, he noted the assignment of guilt without evidence or due process "And once judgment has been rendered against you, the mob starts combing through your past, looking for similar transgressions that might have been missed at the time. I was now told that I'd been creating a toxic environment for years at my workplace" despite the subject never emerging prior to his disagreement with a single influential person. "The constant vigilance on the part of my colleagues and friends did me in. That's why I'm delivering sushi and pizza. Not that I'm complaining. It's honest work, and it's led me to rediscover how to interact with people in the real world. I am a kinder and more respectful person now that I'm not regularly on social media attacking people for not being 'kind' and 'respectful'."

The advocate now expresses deep regret that he "mobbed and shamed people for incidents that became front page news. But when they were vindicated or exonerated by some real-world investigation, it was treated as a footnote by my online community." When the mob had stripped any possible status and caused as much damage as possible, it ventured elsewhere seeking an easier target. "No one ever apologizes for a false accusation, and everyone has a selective memory regarding what they've done." The advocate reviewed his past online behavior that reminded him of once deeply relishing attacking people online and the failure to note his own repeated uncontrolled aggression.

"In my mind I didn't really participate. It was others who took things too far." Nevertheless, facts revealed he was among the worst attackers, his "gleeful savagery" became apparent, and ultimately, following the destruction of his former life, the past online advocate realized how this "two-dimensional" existence had been lacking "human depth." He states, "It is only when we snap out of it, see the world as it really is, and people as they really are, that we appreciate the destruction and human suffering we caused when we were trapped inside."[xxxiv] Social media presents a realistic environmental illusion based on ideas that provoke conflict, emotional responses, and inspires permanent consequences in the real world.[xxxv] One dangerous form of this online aggression targets not just political or social opponents but researchers and scientists as well.

In the past normal scientific debate and reasonable disagreement would occur and facts would ultimately decide the nature of scientific inquiry. However, contingents of modern online aggressors without facts have ideas that cannot survive rational debate and they instead try to discredit and ruin the lives of those considered opponents. Among these attempts to stifle upsetting scientific findings, are relentless threats and online harassment seeking to censor those deemed offensive.[xxxvi] Attacks may extend to family, friends, and anyone connected who does not conform to the selected dogma and so enraptured are some constantly engaged in negative behavior they even claim they do not have to abide by the bounds of science to offer valid criticism, of course, they are wrong.

Dr. Steven Pinker's views that misguided attempts to force social changes will inspire "...regimes to excesses of social engineering." He warns that people seeking to defend political dogma attack verifiable scientific findings and principles to the detriment of all humans. Pinker discusses innate social behaviors that include the "Primacy of family ties, making nepotism and inheritance appealing, a propensity to share based on reciprocity where nonrelatives are concerned, a drive for dominance and a willingness to use violence to attain goals, variation in intelligence (leading to inequalities) and in conscientiousness and antisocial behavior." He notes our proclivity for "biases that deceive people into thinking they are freer, wiser, and more honest than they are. A moral sense, biased toward kin and friends, and linked to ideas of purity, beauty and rank."[xxxvii] This stark reality of biological or social pressures can overwhelm humans because many do not have the will or sufficient ability to defend against overriding influences and in some cases, people irrationally lash out trying to force artificial social constructs to ease their discomfort.

The aggressor's lower brain grows dominant by further engaging in antisocial interactions and this can push some people beyond the limits of reason. Prior cited studies affirm technology's influence over mental processes already geared toward disgust and seeking to dominate a target online the advocate will spend copious amounts of time acting under the power of primal aggression. Curbing this specific problem is necessary if we actually seek to continue scientific progress unimpeded and the offense of political advocates toward scientific research is irrelevant compared to expanding our collective knowledge. While the self-appointed censors of our age do not yet burn books, they do seek to ban them and fear contending public speech under the continued influence of unjustified deeper instincts.

Consistent emotionally distant socialization presents the stage for antisocial behavior and wanton online aggression as the biological desire for a reward grows. Perceived competition guides some to engage with an online challenger and this can drive future negative interactions until they are more important than positive experiences. Negative interactions consistently generate more attention or engagement than positive discussion and this feeds the destructive pattern. The negative feedback cycle becomes a habit and eventually a permanent fixture in regular online interactions that can poison future social relationships. This cycle rewards someone based on increasing outrage and disgust for increasingly less reasonable standards to denigrate an opponent but it ultimately too drives the person deeper into other aggressive social behavior.

A recent study of mental health issues features stark increases in the rates of "negative psychological symptoms" for children born after 1995 during the infancy and rise of online culture. The American Psychological Association found the largest spike in negative symptoms "occurred in 2011, around the same time social media bursts onto the scene." "We found a substantial increase in major depression or suicidal thoughts, psychological distress, and more attempted suicides after 2010, versus the mid-2000s, and that increase was by far the largest in adolescents and young adults." Psychology professor at San Diego State University Jean Twenge states, "These trends are weak or non-existent among adults 26 years and over, suggesting a generational shift in mood disorders instead of an overall increase across all ages."

"The rate of individuals reporting symptoms consistent with major depression in the last 12 months increased 52 percent in adolescents from 2005 to 2017 and 63 percent in young adults age 18 to 25 from 2009 to 2017". "And the rate of young adults with suicidal thoughts or other suicide related outcomes increased a staggering 47 percent from 2008 to 2017."[xxxviii]Among the potential reasons given for large increases in self-destructive behavior is "that digital media use has had a bigger impact on teens and young adults than older adults who tend to have more stable social lives." Thus, without providing the proper stable relationships and coping skills most societies allow young people to delve in a deceptive landscape filled with unforeseen dangers.

In a spiraling environment of mistaken context, anonymous threats, and vicious constant harassment, most can easily guess how this can end violently in some cases. "A perfect storm of factors come together to engender the rudeness and aggression seen in the comments sections of Web pages...First, the (users) are often virtually anonymous, and thus, unaccountable for their rudeness. Second, they are at a distance from the target of their anger- be it the article they're commenting on or another comment on that article- and people tend to antagonize distant abstraction more easily than living, breathing (people)". "Third, it's easier to be nasty in writing than in speech...And because comment-section discourses don't happen in real time, a commenter can write lengthy monologues, which tend to entrench them in their extreme viewpoint." "When you're having a conversation in person...people are talking back and forth and so eventually you have to calm down and listen so you can have a conversation." "Chiming in on a comment threads may even give one a feeling of accomplishment, albeit a false one."[xxxix] Yet while the users might have only detrimental experiences, corporations are in a position to benefit from this constant interaction.

All this activity produces data regarding user patterns for those in a position to benefit from it and seeking to learn every possible bit of useful information, nearly all businesses utilize data collection. This further allows companies to contrast a person's identity with publicly gathered information to create an entire profile that can help gauge your inclinations and how a tailored future message to you or like-minded people needs to be constructed.[xl] Facial recognition software with constant monitoring can help determine audience reactions and expressions to gauge the effectiveness of public events. It also provides groups the ability to use the most engaged supporters and remove less than enthusiastic people from media coverage or even social opportunities. "Consider a recent example from China, where a 'smart eye' system monitors students' engagement and emotions in the classroom. Next, pair this with China's recently launched 'social credit' system" and this system controls access to the best academic schools. "One can easily imagine how improper facial expressions might slide down the slippery slope to become punishable offenses."[xli]

Such technology relies on human designers that can easily misread completely genuine emotions and fabricated displays of virtue. Consider if someone is injured most witnesses react with a pained look of concern naturally despite their connection to a victim. "The pained expression in the observer is greatly intensified if the actor is in eye contact with the observer. The pained expression shown by the observer is now a communicative act, signaling" a recognition of caring and the observer is acknowledged being "a caring person." This example offers situational events and uncontrollable biological distinctions generate most displays of concern until the higher mind processes our actual motivations for doing so. Most do naturally seek to display sympathy but it is the higher mind that decides whether this is a momentary reaction or genuine concern.

The seminal book "Nineteen Eighty-Four" discusses a fictional dystopian future under the control of Big Brother with endless cameras monitoring citizens and legal offenses such as "Facecrime". This "crime" occurs when a person's face displayed "...anything that carried with it the suggestion of abnormality, of having something to hide. In any case, to wear an improper expression on your face...was a punishable offense." "The expressions we see in the faces of others engage a number of different cognitive processes. Emotional expressions elicit rapid responses, which often imitate the emotion in the observed face. These effects can even occur for faces presented in such a way that the observer is not aware of them." However, visual interpretations and environmental factors contrasted with the amount of available information create these expressions. Even the direction and focus of someone's gaze might influence the unconscious assignment of intention by observers despite lacking necessary facts. In one study people that had "invalid" facial expressions and gaze patterns "were rated as less trustworthy" by observers.[xlii] This occurs in part because we cannot fully understand the amount of visual information our brains perceive at one time.

For instance, if we observed a photograph of many similar looking people with smiles and cheering loudly in the face of a different looking lone person standing in opposition to them, most would assume the lone person is being taunted, bullied, or even threatened by the crowd. Yet using Sapolsky's prior methods we might wonder exactly what transpired long before this moment. Did the crowd surround the lone person or did they engage the crowd seeking attention? Did the crowd attack other parties or were other parties intimidating the larger group to incite reactions? Was the large group being violent and vulgar or did they just as prior mentioned cheer and smile? All these factors are part of the reason the original situation may have occurred and redefine the reality of the interaction.

One extreme is a hateful group of detestable people and the other is merely a group not allowing themselves to be intimidated by others using positive expressions of dominance. Further consideration without the proper facts can worsen outrage and lead to public calls for harassment or violence and naturally, many people will seek to confirm their existing biases and identify whichever side appears most sympathetic to be correct. The truth usually rests somewhere between extremely different interpretations and context remains important to realistic assessments of every controversial situation.[xliii] Humans place importance on visual cues, facial expressions, and our reliance on

43

greater information to predict unseen influences paves the way to Facecrime.

The negative use of identification technology is widespread and includes compiling professional, personal, and health information to publicly shame, harass, stalk, and attack "holders of unacceptable sentiments" to anyone taking enough interest. Such people often demand immediate public apologies for being subjectively offended but genuine regret comes naturally based on personal ethics and forced apologies are just fabrications. Apologies are the seeming bonus points in a twisted game some people's brains are playing as they become detached and expressions of outrage become habitual. Certainly, some public outrage is legitimate in the proper circumstances but the aforementioned methods can propagate false, mistaken, and misleading information.

People actively seeking online aggression ceaselessly sacrifice individual reasoning on the altar of collective outrage and such flawed habits never end well. Constant outrage needs conflict and when sufficiently rational targets are lacking any minor infraction will do. Evolving social aggression increases as those engaged in behavior designed to punish others disregard context, internal dissent becomes betrayal, and the need to keep devotees incited grows. A pseudo-religious association can form that begins a freefall toward future aggression and in the worst cases deadly violence. Only the exposure and rejection of these flawed behaviors can prevent them from perpetuating.

Those with greater social status too can affect people in moments of outrage as such influencers succumb to the same negative emotions. Our biological desire for social status can mislead us to embrace the ideas of celebrities or those held in great esteem due to humans eternally heaping social status upon those with the ability to garner desirable attention or dominate others. The easy way to acquire group status uses negative dominant attention that appeals to our lower brain's desire for judging behavior perceived as unacceptable. While a celebrity might have an admirable talent or skill this does not translate into any useful knowledge on a subject of importance. Often, they know less than many people on various subjects because they are too busy practicing their talent and maintaining a fan base. Popularity of ideas can lead observers to confuse value with superficial assertions of knowledge meant only for generating attention.

Finally, there are opportunists who naturally want to garner attention and present themselves as empathetic to victims or the advocates of victim outrage. While legitimate outrage emerges from direct negative treatment, some deceptively use social media to secure more status for themselves without true concern for victims. In atmosphere of perpetual victimhood competition, some who appear to empathize best can gain influence and power due to their persona of limitless humanity. "For example, empathetic expressions of pain are not simply a reflexive response to the sight of pain in another, since they are exaggerated when the empathizer knows he or she is being observed. It seems we want people to know we are empathetic." Humans possess a biological desire to present the proper social behavior to attain and protect their social status and, in several groups, it becomes so coveted many will break with factual analysis to secure further gains. Tribal politics and groupthink remove the need for individuals to reason with context and the collective desire consumes rational self-assessment.

Those obsessed with the outrage cycle seem to forget that online status will never be as fulfilling as personally earned social status. Social media presents a loose hierarchy of ever shifting endorsement and denunciation based on competing user's desires and this can easily lead to conflicts that endure for years based on minor disagreements. All the proper negative influences are present for escalations of depression, aggression, and outrage. Consequently, arguments can quickly devolve to public social media attacks while drawing in additional supporters or detractors and this has in repeated situations lead to threats and acts of violence. Current evidence does not prove that social media itself causes violence; conversely, in some instances it does provide the ground for aggression, harassment, depression, and violence to occur.[xliv] It might cause latent or existing depression to activate or worsen in certain situations based on superficial positive experiences outweighed by negative ones of greater emotional impact. Our natural instincts guide us in some respect and depressive influences may incite anger or worse morph into violence without intervention. Acknowledging the vast positive and negative effects of integrating technology into human society is the first step to developing a means to reduce the undesirable consequences.

Some dishonest people's entire reason for using social media is to generate anger and outrage in others for several purposes. The motivation can range from mere aggressive anonymous entertainment to actively targeting a nation's politics in disinformation campaigns. Several online networks of false identities pushing extremely divisive material to create dissension within all sides of a political debate are reportedly active within at least forty-eight countries. Their methods include one connected group posting hate speech and another coordinating online entity condemning the offensive post and reposting it to "expose" it. Portions of all related material are deemed fake news even when it uses some facts to achieve greater effect, causing greater vitriolic debate and confusion.

However, a misleading post is not seeking to change your opinions but reinforce them to incite the emotions driving a human to lash out. Such posts by design change "what people feel, and the issues themselves have always been whatever people are angriest about. We've seen online influence campaigns; touch on almost everything on which societies profoundly disagree: police brutality, minority rights, gun rights, transgender issues, anti-vaxx, anti-GMO, online privacy concerns, and alleged government corruption. Wedge issues that inflame existing social tensions."[xlv] In some cases, this merely creates limited hostility over a controversial subject, but outrage after outrage likely has a cumulative effect on the minds and emotions of constant users of social media.

The international rise in shootings, terrorism, and suicides with assailants posting repeatedly aggressive, hopeless, and threatening public messages to social media before, during, and after violent episodes infers social media is playing some role in the matter. These inclinations to dominate others have biological origins created long before the influences of environmental technology augmented them. While humans take millennia to slowly adapt and evolve, technological revolutions occur in mere years and now humanity is literally forcing rampant social evolution without understanding all the vital effects of this process. If we blindly continue this evolution without exploring the best options for mitigating further problems, we do so at humanity's peril.

One proponent of environmental influence being the primary cause of violence admits that while biomechanical consequences of some human anatomy do inspire violent behavior, it does not establish that lethal force is an evolutionary imperative shaped by our very nature. Studies do verify that some of our closest primate relatives are extremely violent while others such as gorillas are measurably less violent in comparison to humans.[xlvi] Yet scientists were able to replicate significant violent tendencies and the heritability of aggression in small mammals, especially in lines that were inbred. One study was able to present this was not limited to biological influence but also extended to modification by experience. We should not isolate multiple factors when considering this problem and naturally should consider that more than one influence is required.

Dominance Drive

The evolution of human problem-solving focuses on negative rather than positive traits in weighing vital decisions. The more time a person has to decide an important choice the more critical information is likely gathered as beneficial qualities are usually quickly listed and do not often warrant the attention of significant negative traits. We use this system to form relationships and ultimately it rests upon the individual psychological traits of the two people attempting to form a relationship, their biological compatibility, and the related environment. Among the traits central to successful relationships is a normal dominance drive in males.

Biology presents observable qualities often misattributed to mere psychology or society regarding the need for males to dominate. "In many animal species the mature males fight for social rank and mates. Any pacifistic male that declined to fight would risk failure to reproduce, and its genes for pacifism would be selected out of the population." Many people do not understand that males "in the mammal species possess a 'dominance drive' that impels them to compete for social rank. Sociobiologists have observed further that any female who mated with a male without a dominance drive would risk having sons lacking in reproductive success, and hence would defeat her purpose of passing on her genes". A male's very genetics direct him to assure his reproductive survival by instilling a permanent dominance trait for competition and mating. A female's brain influences her to judge the most dominant mate possessing desired traits among the competitors and this process naturally promotes the survival of dominant genetics and propagation of the human species.

We can observe social competition in males three years and older who received prenatal doses of testosterone which suggests why natural aggression and domination manifests repeatedly in males. The effects of testosterone reportedly increase after challenges to social status thereby generating a greater need for competition and reinforce the instinct for dominating opponents. Yet hormonal levels do not dictate social rank but influence the natural desire to be biologically dominant creatures. Accelerating the progression of societal development and education does not drastically change this pattern but adapts new traits to augment the need for just physical dominance. "In our species too, reproductive success for males is associated with gaining high social rank. Around the world, women tend to prefer a high-ranking, wealthy husband, so men's dominance motivation notably leads to biological success. Thus, dominance behavior relates to marriage and hence to family formation and maintenance."

Intrinsic societal reinforcement pushes males to fight and initiate conflict due to "...its motivational basis, dominance competition-especially among males-is hard to suppress." Wealth is just another biological signal used by humans to demonstrate their impressive reproductive advantages and the vast majority of people respond to such displays. This additionally holds true in the mating rituals of other mammals with extravagant displays ranging from a male peacock's feathers to a male camel's wasting of a vital resources like water in displays of dominance. However, creatures overly fond of displaying resource dominance might endanger the very wealth they rely upon, similar to men who engage in one fight too many and prove less dominant than believed. The creation of nations, accumulating vast resources, timeless art, inspiring music, eternal literature, and technological innovations are just a few of the varied acts males use to gain social rank. Several people do not understand the necessary role of competitive dominance in the establishment of required hierarchy, laws, and societal development.

Yet corrupt dominance that becomes oppressive and no longer benefits a society will eventually fail due to its increasingly unjustifiable costs.[xlvii] Some use criminal or violent means to force domination but a functional civil society punishes these unlawful aggressors and prevents violence with legal force to ensure its stability. In attempts to address the serious issue of illegal aggression, some advocates will drastically overestimate the size of the problem for additional public impact. However properly gauging the size of threats within a population is critical due to hyperbolic politics and emotionally satisfying narratives. What escapes those seeking to blame an entire group for violence is the fractional amount in a group largely responsible for violence in tested populations. One study tracking ten thousand males over nearly three decades born in the United States Midwest found only six percent of those observed "committed 71 percent of homicides, 73 percent of the rapes, and 69 percent of the aggravated assaults attributed to the group."

Another study conducted during 1994 in the American state of Oregon further noted chronic offenders emerged from high crime areas during their teenage years following arrest by the age of fourteen. A related paper studying one European nation determined one percent of the population was responsible for all violent crime convictions.[xlviii] Repeated scientific review supports uncontrolled aggression is limited to a small minority of all men and does not represent all males. Based on international studies attributing criminal behavior to all observed males would be incorrect a majority of the time, it feasibly is a small group that presents the largest propensity for violence and criminal behavior.

True danger instead resides among those anti-social and violent possible future offenders concealed among the majority.

While eighty-seven percent of males cease delinquent behavior by the age of twenty-one, the remainder's behavior accelerates into destructive and violent patterns and these potentially murderous individuals lay hidden among males with normal temperaments. The question becomes how can these future offenders be detected and receive treatment before they become threats? A working hypothesis offered by one scientist predicts that offenders with the greatest risk were those using drugs, left unsupervised, mentally disturbed, or suffering extreme abuse in early childhood. A related study presented at the American Society of Criminology contends that boys arrested by the age of fourteen were nearly twenty times as likely to become "chronic offenders than those who had not, and chronic offenders were 14.3 times more likely to commit violent offenses." "The dangerous few 'are buried within that population of males trying out delinquency. How do you pick them out? Our hypothesis is that those who start earliest are at the highest risk'."

Attempting to predict definitively who the most aggressive offenders in the group are has proved challenging to modern science. One historical mistake was the past reliance of testing seeking males with extra Y-chromosomes or XYY men which some prior believed to be a useful determinate in identifying violent males. However, further research proved it only identified a greater chance of lower intelligence and we should therefore balance action with scientific inquiry. Scientists must resist declaring anything definitive unless such hypotheses present clearly overwhelming verifiable facts or all shall feel the cost of poorly developed methods.

A related puzzle still facing modern science is the determination of what exact trait is most influential in triggering habitually violent or anti-social behavior. Mark Lipsey of Vanderbilt University noted that altering risk factors do not matter if that factor is not the main trigger for unacceptable behavior. It would take several years or longer to determine and deactivate every possible trigger, further it is possible the correct one will remain undiscovered. Lipsey states, "Unfortunately, improvements in predictive models do not necessarily translate into effective intervention strategies".[xlix] One related study contends that curbing antisocial behavior during youth in a minor fraction of adolescent males would allow sizeable reductions in the crime rate. Experts affirmed that job training, family intervention, and rewarding productive attitudes reduced the recurrence of future criminality, yet they are often not as effective as many assume.

Patrick Tolan of the University of Illinois warned about the ineffectiveness of several current anti-crime programs and offers "It is usually hard to imagine that a good idea put into action by well-meaning and enlightened people cannot help...It may seem that any effort is better than nothing. Yet our review and several of the more long-term and sophisticated analyses suggest that both of these assumptions can be dangerously wrong. Not only have programs that have been earnestly launched been ineffective, but some of our seemingly best ideas have led to worsening of the behavior of those subjected to the intervention." The use of social workers, counselors, peer mediation, and neighborhood anti-violence initiatives rarely face assessment for effectiveness and represent a largely used but untested solution. Tolan confirmed, "We do know that locking kids up will not reduce crime and may eventually make the problem worse." There is a feasible increase in anti-social behavior when similar overly aggressive people exist and interact in close proximity and this would support that using incarceration as the first solution, is not effective.

Unfair public criticisms judging all members of any biological group are nonsense, we can repeatedly observe various similar pseudo-scientific claims past humans contrived in the service of beliefs without substantial evidence. Advocates in modern society calling for punitive action have attempted to label all male culture as toxic, and they obviously remain ignorant that a slight minority of all men commit most violence decried. It seems as if some may seek to inflate the size of the problem to generate more attention, influence, and funding but this does not address the over ten percent of all modern violent crime that females commit.[1] Nor is there much public limelight, sympathy, or advocacy for males abused by females.

The Los Angeles Times reports that disbelief is the common response to husbands claiming spousal abuse by their wives but over two hundred academic studies found that in mutually violent relationships "women were as likely as men to be the aggressors". While females are assumed to be a lesser physical threat, they can employ weapons, poison, and various other methods and strategies that quickly overcome any liability.[li] Societal taboos against harming women in some cases have also prevented men from defending themselves despite possessing an overwhelming physical advantage. Even if females had the exact statistics of males this still proves a minority among them were responsible for most crime, several females constituting a serious problem does not make female culture toxic. Attempting to label the entire male culture toxic ignores the overwhelming facts and the stabilizing role of most males defending the human species.

We must rely upon nothing less than unconditional precision if we seek to address the true origin of the violence problem because false allegations target innocent people based on flawed ideas. The dangers of falsely identifying potential offenders with imprecise methods created by the prior XYY testing debacle reveals there are varying possibilities for the strongest determining factor of chronic aggression. While observing violence appears to increase the risk of a child repeating what it regularly witnesses, it is not a definitive cause of violence and some factors are exceedingly more common. This would also challenge popular claims of blaming media or entertainment for containing violence, there is no clear distinction that witnessing fictional violence consistently inspires real violence. Most people do not commit violence by just observing or experiencing it and some actually become more committed to maintaining lawful peace and the reduction of violence from exposure.

Determining a single overriding factor or persistent combination of the same factors still has proven elusive and many will leap to conclusions without definitive proof. Our hopes may lie in early detection methods that could additionally provide beneficial financial results with one American study claiming "For every 1 percent we reduce the violence, we save the country 1.2 billion."[lii] One suggested reduction method is asking parents to evaluate their young child's behavior and attitudes coupled with neurological testing, psychological therapy, and pharmaceutical treatment. Yet we must be vigilant that our desire to correct potentially violent people does not overcome the need for respecting human rights. Some worry early detection methods have and still could possibly condemn misdiagnosed non-violent children or those who had tendencies for aggression but had not yet committed a violent offense to forced treatment. The ethical differences are critical between detecting high-risk people while offering treatment and making such treatment compulsory. Evolving politics, emotional public responses, and past mistakes present an environment where these concerns are valid.

Murder and Psychopaths

A modern survey of five thousand people from around the world revealed that ninety-one percent of males and eighty-four percent of female respondents "thought about ending somebody else's life...Though we might like to think that murderers are either pathological misfits or hardened criminals".[liii] The report concludes stating most who commit murder appear normal until the moment they chose to kill because the most loving mother, attentive father, unassumingly sweet children, supportive aunts and uncles, and kind grandparents has within them a potential murderer. The seductive urges of our deeper brain can influence our higher consciousness into justifying these methods to cope with employing them. Contrarily, some people do not require a coping mechanism because they do not feel any human sympathy and remorse.

Centuries ago, people classified a psychopath as someone possessing the ability to distinguish right from wrong but lacking any normal moral compass. Modern data suggests psychopaths "enjoy what the rest of us consider abhorrent and heinous. They recognize the harmful consequences of their acts, but they're incapable of feeling remorse, and concern for the victim is completely absent. They are not immoral; they're amoral."[liv] Contrary to popular fiction, many psychopaths do not physically harm victims but cause social and emotional damage by using manipulation, intimidation, and threats to secure their agendas. A psychopath will be deceptive, persuasive, does not accept responsibility for their failures, and makes excuses to avoid blame. Psychopaths are not usually delusional but often significantly overestimate their own merits and power based on their unfounded narcissism. Notably only some psychopaths display violent behavior and circumstances triggering this descent can vary as much as the weapons used.

Author Thomas McDade reports in his book "The Annals of Murder" the first recorded murder in the Americas following the establishment of English rule was a man shot during 1630. The employment of poison in domestic murders was routine, "It might have been antimony in the lemonade, laudanum in the coffee, morphine in the whiskey, or strychnine in the sugar bowl. Arsenic could be dusted over oysters...even steeped in chamomile tea. Poison was everywhere in early America, and poisoners could buy it anywhere."[lv] A former resident of a mental asylum employed the first mail bomb seeking to kill his former asylum's superintendent in 1854. The motives for these various deadly instances spanned from reportedly petty insults and extend to deep enduring psychosis but all these roads might quickly lead to violence.

Howard Unruh, the first mass murderer in United States history was no exception when several factors ranging from petty to significant caused him to lash out. Unruh fumed after failing to meet a male companion, was already paranoid about his neighbors, and incensed because someone removed his newly installed gate. Investigators reported Unruh had contemplated killing his neighbors for years due to arguments, insults, and his existing undiagnosed emotional problems. The morning of Labor Day 1949, he left his New Jersey apartment with a German Luger prior claimed during World War II and killed thirteen people. Unruh without comment shot the owner of a local shoe store then executed the proprietor of a barbershop and his young customer. He proceeded down the block randomly firing into buildings and even called out to a shocked onlooker before gunning him down in the street. The killer next murdered an entire family including a grandmother inside a local apartment building. Unruh then walked down the street killed four motorists and fired into one car's windshield missing a small child but killing its two female relatives in the front seat. He proceeded to shoot a mother and her toddler son before completing his rampage by wounding two members of another family.

Officials attributed Unruh's transformation from irritable veteran to cold-blooded executioner on undiagnosed post-traumatic stress disorder from his wartime service.[lvi] While mass murder in 1940s America was a major aberration in public behavior, such actions presently occur internationally with alarming regularity. Subsequent mass murder cases too repeatedly feature mental illness, severe trauma; and reveal that violent experiences potentially distort our natural aggressive tendencies. Unruh from his biology, environmental traumas, paranoia, and constant perceived agitation had become psychopathic. He is a case study of the most dangerous minority on Earth undertaking a series of horrific events that others increasingly repeat and this rise in psychopathic behavior leaves a growing trail of victims.

Neuroscientist James Fallon has studied the biological origins of human conduct in the brains of psychopaths extensively for decades. He subsequently discovered that his father's relatives included several murderous people that exhibited action indicating a potential for increased violent tendencies in his own biology. Using past conduct and positron emission tornography (PET) imaging to support his hypothesis, Fallon presented images of a brain with low frontal cortex activity, one of the biological traits believed to indicate reduced ethical behavior. The orbital cortex limits the human brain's impulses and instinctual desires of the amygdala, the center of human aggression. Failure in the frontal cortex resulting from biology or injury surrenders control to the "area of the brain that drives your id-type behaviors, which is rage, violence, eating, sex, drinking."

Using the samples provided by a number of his family members Fallon determined that all but one member of his family was completely with the normal range of activity. The only abnormal reduced prefrontal activity in the images Fallon analyzed were those contained in his own scan and he states to an interviewer "If you look at the PET scan, I look just like one of those killers". Another trait in only Fallon's biology was the MAO-A gene and Fallon notes it is "also known as the 'warrior gene' because it regulates serotonin levels in the brain. Serotonin affects your mood--think Prozac--and many scientists believe if you have a certain version of the warrior gene, your brain won't respond to the calming effects of serotonin." [lvii] Two of the important biological factors leading to violence and criminality were present in James Fallon yet he was missing a final key trait present in violent criminals, severe childhood trauma.

Fallon unlike several noted violent criminals had loving parents that raised him with ethics and he did not suffer permanent damage from repeated psychological and social traumas. Essentially his good parents, positive social upbringing, and education allowed Fallon to overcome the inherent violent biological potential lurking within him. To defend the mind's lacking defense against the development of psychopathic habits it is possible to introduce new positive structures during childhood. Supportive relationships with family and friends erected upon a consistent and ethical foundation to deny instinctually violent impulses establishes constructive habits. Developing adequate psychological defenses would likely require years of teaching acceptable behavior, psychiatric consultation, and experiences that reinforce sympathy and empathy in a child. Positive behavior patterns and repetition can reduce the propensity for violence but this holds true conversely as well. Negative reinforced patterns over extended periods generate a nearly identical emergence of savagery in lower mammals and humans.

A common diagnosis that could trigger excessive violent behavior in people is "Borderline Personality Disorder (BPD)" which includes "emotional instability, anxiety, and psychotic-like symptoms where those afflicted can suddenly become very paranoid or suspicious of others." BPD can manifest by causing an individual to possess little empathy for the emotions of any other human beings and some attribute it to chemical imbalances. A set of circumstances in the right sequence could quickly trigger the proper environment suitable for serial murder if "...there is a situational or environmental trigger for these outbursts, the killing could become serial. This would be in contrast to psychopathic serial killers".[lviii] However, an even smaller percentage of psychopaths are not just violent but utterly murderous and without remorse.

Serial killers are capable of monstrous deeds and represent the lower brain's domination of behavior in the context of violent tendencies dominating human morality. An important distinction between a regular psychopath and serial killers is while many serial killers are psychopaths; most violent psychopaths are not serial killers. While the average person can lash out during instances of isolated rage, serial killers display consistently murderous behavior that does not rely on prior interaction or justification. They lack empathy, possess a low resting heart rate, and possibly reduced prefrontal gray matter or activity in the region controlling functions of the higher brain. Such defects are required traits to allow the deeper brain's instincts to dominate behavior and thus our animalistic tendencies to ravage normally functioning biological defenses. The public often inspects and discusses serial killers but such psychopaths are but a small fraction of humanity. They are seemingly a permanent fixture in popular culture and media because they present the darkest reaches possible in all of us.

Researchers seek to determine how we can recognize the early signs of deep psychosis and prevent the development of biological and social dysfunction into active violent psychotic episodes. Experts hope for more progress toward a future solution or means to blunt destructive social behavior and mental instability but science has yet to make significant advances in determining comprehensive treatment. Perhaps most troubling is that no cure for adult psychopaths yet exists and will likely be soon forthcoming. Nevertheless, violence is not merely limited to mentally disturbed individuals but a topic of great interest to some groups repeatedly utilizing it.

Collective Violence

Collective violence refers to large groups employing destructive tactics such as international battles, assassination, and genocide. Local, regional, or national groups will engage in violence because it remains infinitely easier to destroy an enemy than attempt mutually beneficial coexistence. To satisfy our mind's basest impulses world leaders have mixed our biological capacity for violence with geopolitics and the results have been dire. The same aggressive impulses fueling heroism in defensive military wars can transform to brutality during illegal political interventions and when the aggressor's biological triggers for hostility merge with militant egotism, the unjustifiable becomes easier. Failing to abide legal and fair rules of conduct and engagement blurs the lines of moral action and repeatedly leads to humanitarian disasters.

Brooding underneath complex diplomacy, brutality, and political sentiment for increased domination is part of the lower brain with its territorial responses feeding our desires for increased control of the world around us by any means necessary. We have provided the lower brain with all the innovations of our age and humanity should rightly tremble at the possibilities for violence on a mass scale. Empowered by modern advancements in weaponry and uncontrolled access to armaments, collective violence has a greater effect currently than its prior historical counterparts did. The once angry mob that could burn down a town and kill its rich inhabitants now can develop a chemical or explosive attack that might endanger the entire population of a large metropolis. One news report on the matter states nearly one hundred and ten million people died from wars in the twentieth century and based on related estimates this represents more historical warfare deaths than all prior historical periods.[lix]

"An enormous amount of resources (financial, environmental, and human) has been devoted to the science of killing...by governments, arms manufacturers, international terrorist networks, and paramilitary groups." "This is not to suggest that actions taken by members of these disparate groups are morally equivalent, but certain of the behavioral dynamics involved are common." We cannot permit intuitive tendencies for violence because they utterly clash with several aspects of civil modern life and prevent stability. Even justified self-defense must enlist methods of preventative social domination but humans should only resort to physical violence if it becomes necessary. According to several biological studies, humans consistently have maintained social order with the threat and use of justified violence.

Essentially despite the negative effects of violence, humans possess "neural circuits of rage and violence because we need them. As a species we needed deadly violence to obtain food, to protect ourselves, our family, our group, and unfortunately we still need them today." Acceptable repressive violence can stop violent domestic unrest according to laws and its mere threat can be a stabilizing factor that "benefits society at large". A supporting scientist offers, "We don't hate violence, we hate the wrong kind of violence. When it is the right kind we get all excited, we leap to see it, we hand out medals, we disproportionately vote for and mate with the people who are best at that, when it's the right kind of violence we love it."[lx] Collectively accepted legal punishment keep most concerned with arrest, imprisonment, loss of resources, and several detrimental consequences that result from lawless behavior. This "organized violence is founded on the same neurocircuitry of aggression wired into the human brain of every individual" and to ban all violence would necessitate the removal of necessary defensive violence as well.[lxi]

A contextual question is what constitutes necessary violence? The question can be disturbing because those employing violent, coercive, or retaliatory methods can enjoy a temporary positive result. Yet impulsively aggressive tactics ignore the longer-term costs beyond temporary repression of the chosen target and the backlash resulting from collective violent action can linger indefinitely. Extended consequences may involve the upheaval of the repressing authority or the destruction of an offending group and this creates a problem that may dwarf the original risk. Any group's leadership seeking preemptive violent action will usually present a narrative to support its "positive" aspects and claim that failing to do so offers "dire" repercussions. Thus, what justifications and means are employed becomes critical to distinguish between justified legal violence and illegal repressive aggression. Whether this is a war, political assassination, terrorist bombing, or gang ambush, the results are largely the same for the victims. [lxii]

Consider the persistent bloodshed of various countries victimized by modern terrorism; some groups not satisfied with killing just their fellow citizens often invade other nations as well. Nearly every continent on Earth has been the target of imported and domestic terrorism based on political and religious groups seeking to intimidate others. Yet they fail to understand the urges within their brain guiding unfounded justifications for violent aggression and the ultimate futility of such actions. Needless use of lethal violence is the road to self-destruction, because such behavior will usually lead to the perpetrator's arrest, imprisonment, or death under the lawful structure of most societies. Yet this does not dissuade misguided people acting in destructive ways they believe are justified and to prevent such acts the origin of their unfounded ideas must be inspected.

Some religious parables offer great moral and philosophical value but faith too has been repeatedly misused to support nearly any violent crime imaginable. Religions formed in part as a way to set limitations upon individuals under the shared banner of a dogma that provides a unified structure and ideal under which to operate. Unfortunately, it too allows the leadership to dominate the faithful with often-unverifiable supernatural claims and most popular religious texts command their followers to strike down unbelievers that oppose the express mandates of the group. Modern terrorists of nearly every major religious group attempt to justify the misunderstood impulses of human biology and society with religion and some aspire to wage eternal war. Anyone who does not share his or her violent beliefs or even a different brand of the same faith becomes an enemy in this mindless surrender to aggressive violence. As the extremist mind slips further into embracing violence greater trauma develops and causes added mental and emotional distortion.

Even utilizing extreme violence when lawful often has traumatic effects despite how battle hardened the subject and damage resulting from exposure to severe periods of violence is quite common. Functional human beings when thrust into an unrelenting environment such as war often must use even irrational means to cope with the brutality they must participate in and experience. The mindset of multiple soldiers in war can offer insights to what undertaking violence in the name of a cause might yield. Nations call upon citizens to carry out wars in their name but most seemingly ignore the expansive mental and emotional price combat troops must pay.

In times of war, the human mind faces gruesome violence often beyond its control and seeks to justify the aggression employed using any plausible reason. This justification process is observable in the stories and emotions of soldiers who served in wartime such as former Marine William Broyles that described the allure of lethal conflict when he stated "...there were dozens of reasons why combat might be attractive, even pleasurable.

Comradeship with its bittersweet absorption of the self within the group, appealed to some fundamental human urge. And then--in contrast--there was the awesome power conferred upon individuals for war. For men combat was the male equivalent of childbirth: it was the 'initiation in the power of life and death'. Broyles had little to say about the 'life' aspect, but argued that the thrill of destruction was irresistible."

"A bazooka or an M-60 machine gun was a 'magic sword' or a 'grunt's Excalibur". "Killing had a spiritual resonance and an aesthetic poignancy. Slaughter was 'an affair or great and seductive beauty'. For combat soldiers, there was as much mechanical elegance in an M-60 machine gun as there was for medieval warriors decorated swords. Aesthetic tastes were highly personal: some Marines favored the silent omnipotence of napalm, while others (such as Broyles) preferred white phosphorous because it exploded with a fulsome elegance, wreathing its target in intense and billowing smoke, throwing out glowing red comets tailing brilliant white plumes."[lxiii] The minds of soldiers constructed a merciless beauty in undertaking violence based on politics and national security; these disturbing feelings of beauty largely sought to explain the violent primal urges that manifest in war.

Nor is this attribution of beauty to violence constrained to Western military actions, one story of past violence within Indonesia attempted to render brutal savagery into the sublime. During the 1960s, a right wing Indonesian nationalist group conducted a coup that would eventually lead to the death of hundreds of thousands of enemy civilians. One academic investigating encountered multiple stories of right-wing death squads hunting down entire villages with a local orchestra in tow. Another academic later questioned a member of the death squads about the purpose of these strange musical observers and learned that orchestra members were required to make the event "more beautiful". Seemingly, people can find supposed "beauty" in violent actions they perceive as justified even if they morally are not.[lxiv]

Following wars diplomacy too could be lethal if the parties violated peace treaties established upon a future threat of violence and just the perception of a diplomatic breach could result in lethal consequences for a political captive. "The Aztecs, Carthaginians, and Greeks sacrificed captives; peoples from Iceland, Tanzania, and Margi held prisoners of war for ransom."[lxv] Women faced captivity via forced marriage to secure political alliances and beneficial trade agreements in repeated nations from all levels of a society. European and Middle Eastern nations used forced religious conversion, execution, ransom, and political captives in some periods to cement alliances with a person's safety weighed against diplomatic violations.

The human brain guides our decision-making process by individually perceived justifications to use lethal force and we are more predisposed to using violence if we attach danger to a specific target. "Study of the brain using simulated killing found reactions occurred differently based upon the victim's threat status. Guilt correspondingly rose when the subject believed the murder was not fully justified, targeting an enemy soldier merely activates a portion of the brain used for spatial recognition. Contrarily, when civilians were targeted multiple portions of the brain reacted marking a significant difference in the process based on the context of target status. While ultimately shooting either target kills them, an enemy soldier represents a target acceptable under lawful combat and illegally killing civilians provoked a greater chance for remorse. "In all of us it's clear that murder's neural roots and moral roots are deeply entangled."[lxvi]

While our brain can often distinguish the difference between enemy combatants and civilians the line grows less clear as further violent engagements paired with survival instincts dehumanize the enemy. Soldiers must endure the horrors of war and this saddles them with a great emotional burden concealed from most civilians. Greater periods of defying normal social behavior can disrupt a person's ability to cope with stressful influences often compounded by posttraumatic stress disorder or suicidal tendencies. Extended terms of military deployment in hostile areas without sufficient logistical or public support can increase the possibility of soldiers experiencing violent or depressive symptoms. Thus, we must justify to ourselves the need to kill someone for survival but increased periods of trauma can disrupt our ability to distinguish between defensive and aggressive violence.

Justification for immoral violence increases by demonizing the chosen target or group as evil, inherently flawed, and wholly inhuman. If one uses these hyperbolic standards for extended durations, violence is likely soon to follow with none of the negative mental or social associations developed to prevent such action. Labeling a target or group irredeemable "naturally has a profound effect on one's readiness to attack them, or to explore peaceful alternatives. History demonstrates that participants who are taught that it is essential to act against members of an opposing group even if such action may cause pain to the innocent are likely willing to do so." If humans make constant excuses for the use of irrational violence, they normalize it and the chances of its meaningful reduction becomes exponentially more difficult. Eventually such permitted violence could become a permanent fixture within a culture and forever preclude it from peaceful interactions with those who oppose it in nearly any matter of importance.

Spikes of violence consistently occurring during the progression of human society support that people are usually in a state of environmental stress and conflict. Among the notable periods was a rise in violence during the Dark Ages into years near the Renaissance when reportedly ten percent of people died in wars and religious crusades amidst vast periods of rampant disease. This is wholly understandable due to the pervasive loss of basic infrastructure, the absence of scientific inquiry, political upheaval, and religious inspired violence. These numbers culminated at the time of the New World's discovery with twenty-five percent of human deaths ascribed to other "civilized" people. One explanation for widespread violence during this period is a society's authorities sanctioning invasion without consideration to any long-term ramifications of using violence. The conquest and exploitation of the New World had express approval from religious leaders and thus by extension a deity's support was lent to conquest. Seeking to fill their coffers all manner of religious groups and monarchs gave aspiring conquistadors license to indiscriminately murder, rape, and steal whatever their hearts desired in the name of a nation and god. This resulted in the death or permanent crippling of native societies and was not limited to the West.

The East as well is full of brutal subjugation such as the expansive Mongol Empire dominating a huge portion of the known world that claimed the lives of at least eleven million people. The Khans simultaneously assimilated or wiped opposing tribes and armies from existence but Western leaders who condemned the Mongols for rapine savagery allowed their own representatives to use these exact methods in the New World. As Europeans colonized the Americas, the eventual discovery of lethal native ceremonies that demanded human hearts and innocent children would confirm that societal brutality was already prevalent before the European domination had begun. All these competing human factions were long versed in murder and it was among the common methods once adapted for survival that spiraled out of control. Waves of new immigrants challenged the population growth and influence of colonizing groups and violence between them expanded to overtake some imperial colonies. To dominate rival populations some influential leaders convinced devotees that specific cultural identities have intrinsic moral superiority. Ranging from fascist strongmen to communist tyrants all manner of influence has and will be utilized by the dishonest to promote the abominable.

Warring nations like some criminal groups export violence for both defensive justified reasons and unjustified acts of aggression in the cause of national security interests. Such wars are often reliant on intelligence assessment and corresponding national agencies play a role in providing information to leaders about the best military approach in dealing with other nations. The unseen hand of intelligence is often unmasked years later as historical declassification occurs and this finger on the scales of policy is considerable. Repeated unjustified interference by intelligence groups can erode not just the independence of a government but also the care in which they employ violent means. To secure desired agendas such groups use calls for action to inspire supporters and drive public opinion with appeals to patriotism, authority, and supposedly righteous causes. However, this intrinsic aggression and resulting hostility is not limited to governments but also invaded some realms of public advocacy.

Certain groups desire to justify and incite the use of violence by other people despite lacking a rational justification and others find themselves manipulated into justifying illegal actions by calling it brave and attaching a group status to the violation of laws. The pseudo-religious dogmas of supposedly "moral" social groups have notable terminology and concepts equivalent to the average religion. Take for instance the religious idea of original sin; this asserts that despite being guilty of nothing humans enter the world tainted by sin. The concept presents a largely common sin inheritance of sorts that renders people eternally flawed without religious absolution. There is no shortage of religious officials and new age gurus willing to help you "fix" this problem for the right size donations.

Now compare original sin to the modern concept of "privilege" asserted by secular advocates who insist all those in a marked group are intrinsically guilty of oppressing people by the mere act of existing. While some details in the exact process of assigning unjustified blame might differ, the biased system without a reasonable chance of redemption is the same. You are determined flawed and can never be a positive influence unless you purge your "sin" by succumbing to the dogma of the group. It is a seeming attempt to use pseudo-religious arguments in secular politics and this fervent belief has led to instances of escalating unlawful violence repeatedly. These attacks knowingly or unknowingly encroach upon the fundamental right to equal free speech that all people should enjoy in every society.

Reporter Katrina Trinko offers, "If you're using...privilege to shut people up, you're the problem...In fact, we should be judging speech-and speakers-by their content, not their racial background, gender, sexual orientation, IQ, or any other host of factors." "Yet worryingly, we seem to be moving to a world where it's your characteristics, not your thoughts that determine if you will be heard." Trinko further displays examples of the inconsistency by which different people judge such concepts of "privilege" and ignore other advantages they possess in favor of their assumptions. Strikingly, a recent study from Princeton and Yale Universities supports that it is those advocating ideas of privilege that often trying to appear empathetic will intentionally mask their own competence to submit to those considered disadvantaged.[lxvii] The foundation of unspoken patronizing overcompensation is feasibly misplaced guilt and seeking ally status. It fuels attempts to silence those who disagree because it likely triggers the fear and disgust mechanisms when such ideas face public challenge. This need to decry someone opposing a belief and publicly mark them a rival group member can lead to erroneous assumptions.

During one notable more recent example, a black female news analyst and gravelly voiced male interviewer were debating and the female journalist implied that her male interviewer could not understand and did not face the challenges she did. The female analyst claimed that "white privilege" skewed his ideas and he could not understand the plight of a black person, thus based on a biological claim of some mystical ability to experience what others cannot the analyst declared the "oppressor bias" she had constructed was a suitable answer. However, a single fact destroyed these claims when the interviewer revealed he too was black and this would later cause his guest to apologize for her attempt at lecturing others. Because the male host disagreed, the analyst made an invalid assumption based on her desire to be right but was unconcerned with being factual.[lxviii] Many find the instinctive desire to demean the ideas of those we hold biases against irresistible but the derivation of privilege is not skin color but wealth, status, and social influence.

Political tribalism has increasingly expanded the construction of fringe doctrines to justify violence by advocates promoting societal conflict via clashes in the name of "social justice" or "nationalism" but these opposing groups all revel in the same unjustified aggression. These violent actions are not accomplishing valuable progress but merely committed by people who desire to be aggressive and want attention. They are similar to a screaming child breaking toys that is determined the world shall hear them despite what disruption they might cause. Indeed, nonviolent protest is necessary in justified situations of clear unreason to initiate equitable changes in a society but groups allowing members to commit illegal brutality without expelling them become complicit in that violence.

We can fight these disturbing ancient urges but it requires the cooperation of a society to curb this behavior with all the tools at hand. Humans eventually must confront that despite all the high-minded accomplishments of our species, we too are barely civilized based on a proclivity to strike down those who we determine to be a threat to our goals, resources, and territory. The political desires of various nations and social movements have inspired the use of organized violence repeatedly in the course of world history because the urge to kill is a mammalian instinct older than humanity itself. We must resist our biology's negative inclinations and be willing to disengage from social patterns fueling irrational feelings that lead to violence. Perhaps an inspection of the only two superpowers that existed during the twentieth century may reveal the depths of humanity's aggression.

CHAPTER 3:

NOTABLE AMERICAN VIOLENCE

"Under well-settled legal principles, lethal force against a valid military objective, in an armed conflict, is consistent with the law of war and does not, by definition, constitute an assassination."
- J. Johnson, US Secretary of Homeland Security

With our knowledge of human territoriality, add the new dimensions of national boundaries and corridors of influence to our perceived spheres of control. The ancient neural connections that commanded us to defend a small cave or family dwelling have expanded to millions of square miles. Threats to vital resources located great distances from the nation claiming them and just perception of disrespect has inspired centuries of subterfuge and clandestine sparring. Few nations have risen quickly to the forefront of power or enduring domination and the path leading to the United States of America's founding details the resulting clash of multiple civilizations in a history fraught with aggression and violence.

When two societies collide, war is the outcome and one study reports in the past thirty-four hundred years as a species we have been at peace for about eight percent of that entire period. A group's organizational capability, technological advances, and the environment in which battles transpire often dictate the results. North America with its loosely associated native tribes, abundance of land, and vast natural resources proved ripe for centuries of colonization. "Europeans came to the New World with the Old

World motivation of conquest pure and simple. In the way that the Romans took over most of Europe two thousand years ago, and the Normans conquered Anglo-Saxon England in 1066, conquest was the primary incentive."[lxix] This barbarity carried on to the descendants of those prior conquering foreign lands across the Atlantic and evolved into policies of permanent legal subjugation.

One stark difference between the conventions of colonizing European powers and existing Native American tribes was complex property laws. Native American tribes encountering settlers did not anticipate the consequences of European trade agreements or resulting disputes to provide the excuse for military aggression. North American tribal society had defined personal ownership of objects, animals, and even people but their system of land ownership was communal. This key difference allowed competing factions to make deals without the consent of the entire tribe and would expand the future conflict between these cultures. As time passed the basic desire of colonizing forces to acquire power and territory overcame any chance for lasting peace or fair trade.

Slavery did exist in the American continents for centuries but contrary to some modern opinions, the United States did not begin or massively expand this inhuman machine of oppression. The instinctual desire for subjugating other human beings to benefit a society has been a constant practice for millennia based on mammalian tendencies. Historian Christina Snyder notes "Slavery has existed in some form in nearly every society from hunter-gatherers to farmers to industrialized nations". "Slavery is not peculiar, nor is the fact that Native Americans practiced it."[lxx] They practiced captivity for several reasons including to prevent future wars by the forced marriage and subjugation of losing tribes. It was not a "static institution" but transitioned based on their needs such as during the era before European colonists arrived in which "rival chiefs vying for power went to war and took prisoners, exploiting these conquered enemies to enhance the power of their own ruling lineages."

This Native American activity mirrors significant reasoning used in other Western societies to overthrow and oppress weaker groups. Notably due to the Ice Age and immigration from Asia to North America via later inaccessible land connections early American society and the rest of the world almost never made contact. In all but a few exceptions, this civilization developed independently but decided upon largely the same means of dominating the conquered. This separately contrived but similar method could denote our common biological tendencies coupled with vastly different environments and social development. To assume slavery is a unique or singular trait of the United States is to ignore a millennium of history.

"Following the European invasion of America, Native people experienced demographic collapse owing to epidemic diseases and subsequent incorporation into a global economy that valued Indian slaves. Both factors encouraged them to capture and sell unprecedented numbers of captives." Essentially, they sold any captives surviving disease into slavery as the European slave trade increased, similar to the practice of some international tribes. Snyder reports "Captivity, which both colonizer and Native people practiced included a broad range of forms extending from temporary bondage to hereditary slavery. Though sexual relationships, adaption, hard work, military service, or escape, captives could enhance their status". "Some people, including African Americans who lived among the Seminoles, were neither slave nor free but lived perpetually in between." Multiple Europeans countries and Native Americans set up a captivity hierarchy that slowly developed into later more encompassing "racial slavery".[lxxi]

For Native Americans captivity might only signify a diplomatic hostage via marriage but extended to racial slavery of outsiders considered to exist merely for the material or social enrichment of the person that controlled them. Unlike in European colonies Native Americans did not develop any racial component linked to the enslaved, anyone of any culture might end up in captivity or enslavement. Some Native tribes later equated racial traits to slave status likely from the centuries of prior European religious encroachment mixed with imperial scientific ignorance. "Nor did modern Western ideas about freedom resonate with Native people."

"In the Native view, as in many African societies, the opposite of slavery was not freedom: the opposite of slavery was kinship." Many Native American tribes supported the most important bond was with one's clan. "Members of the clan reckoned that they were all related, all have descended from an ancient, mythic ancestor, such as Wind, Bear, Panther, or Wolf. Clans were ranked relative to one another, and clan rank as well as one's position within his or her clan figured into status." This harkens back to the basic desire of all mammals to compete for status and place themselves and others in a defined hierarchy. As captives or kin increased the rank and status of their clan, each leader of the benefitting clan gained power or influence.

However, captives had no established place or status in the kinship arrangement and while this granted more freedom than formal slavery it left that captive vulnerable to the whims of anyone with status. "Native people doubted that outsiders were fully human, and they certainly did not believe all people were endowed with natural rights...oral traditions suggest that Native people did not believe every being appearing in the form of a person was actually human. They labeled outsiders "accursed nothings" or were associated with the lowest members of the animal world effectively reducing them to less than human. [lxxii] These natural social developments of favoring tribe over new arrivals set the stage for placing value on the subjugation of outsiders and several modern concepts of slavery do not consider the human bondage used before any European came to the Americas.

Other forms of servitude and slavery began centuries before the United States existed under multiple European powers (France, England, Portugal, Spain, and the Netherlands) that contracted and traded indentured servants in the colonial Americas. English imperial officials used the widespread European practice of indentured servitude as a means of production. Seeking to escape bleak prospects, repay substantial debts, or begin a new life in North America masses of people were forced or accepted legal bondage for themselves and their families as servants. Unlike a fair contract between a working person with all due rights and a single employer, this was nothing less than ceding most personal freedom to another person legally until repayment was complete. Surrendering our self-determination to another person is dehumanizing, it rightfully inspires deep bitterness in any but the most submissive of people that do not value personal choice. Yet servitude in nearly all cases had a legal time limit that vanished when the practice transitioned into slavery.

"One of the places we have the clearest views of that 'terrible transformation' is the colony of Virginia. In the early years of the colony, many Africans and poor whites--most of the laborers came from the English working class--stood on the same ground. Black and white women worked side by side in the fields. Black and white men who broke their servant contract were equally punished." Servants did enjoy room and board and several made provisions for them to receive an end of contract reward "known as 'freedom dues' which usually included a piece of land and supplies, including a gun. Black skinned or white-skinned, they became free."

English colonists usually enslaved "non-Christians" without regard to racial background and European countries possessed slaves long prior to the colonization of the American continents. Nevertheless, slavery was not originally a lifelong sentence and some could attain freedom by conversion to Christianity. "The first Virginia colonists did not even think of themselves as 'white' or use that word to describe themselves. They saw themselves as Christians or Englishmen, or in terms of their social class." The inception of servitude paired with gaining status would render an environment for the development of English slavery in the American colonies.

It became clear following the death of a significant numbers of white European indentured servants their pale skin and weak resistance to some foreign diseases would repeatedly prevent them from surviving their contract's terms. This proved a financial detriment and waste of resources to the contract holders and they decided that darker skinned people with greater physical constitution fared much better in the southern American climate. Africans could be abducted or purchased in tribal held areas unlike English citizens and were not subject to imperial law. Based in part on financial decisions, the use of religious justification, and political invectives, the English and other nations would increase the amount of Caribbean and African slaves and financially profit from these ideological revisions. The human bondage trade became an institutional weapon used by imperial powers against black people.

Perhaps most striking are the often-unknown legal actions that rendered black indentured servants into legal slaves and set precedent for others to expand the definition of servant into slave. European servants often agreed to contractual servitude but several traders compelled African servants into contracts. Anthony Johnson was one such African who unlike many others in colonial Virginia was able to prosper and eventually owned a tobacco farm and his own black indentured servants. Johnson purchased three indentured servants during sixteen forty and John Punch was one of these people. Punch was reportedly an African that following his prior escape from bondage was sentenced to servitude the rest of his natural life and the "next year Massachusetts became the first colony to legally recognize slavery."

Legal prohibitions on freedmen purchasing land were introduced as former indentured servants gained land rights, drew on local resources, and competed with former contract owners. Those prior held in servitude grew angry because they could not even acquire property with their hard-earned money and this led to a riot that was responsible for incinerating colonial Jamestown. While the disgruntled freedmen often remained, servants requiring expensive new contracts could flee and there was an endless variation of different people among the indentured. This made racial slavery even more attractive because according to one media report "...slaves, especially ones you could identify by skin color, could not move on and become free competitors."

When another of Johnson's "servants" John Casor disagreed with him over the completion of his contract, Johnson took the matter to a Virginia Court in the 1650s. "The court sided with Johnson, who claimed that Casor was his slave for life...It was a watershed moment in the history of institutional slavery" in Virginia.[lxxiii] With this public claim and second legal act, the stage was set for lifelong servitude to be unleashed and develop into the reprehensible form of bondage that over a century later would dominate the southern United States. What religious conversion or contract service once could dissolve became a deeper unchangeable system of status not based on finance or religion but race. Colonial Virginia would legalize slavery and by 1662, the colony "decided all children born in the colony to a slave mother would be enslaved." These increasingly abominable legal provisions would create an enduring underclass and allow slave owners to refill the slave populations without having to expend as many resources.

When Anthony Johnson died his land and property was seized because "he was a negroe and by consequence an alien". The colony declared all "servants imported and brought in this County...who were not Christians in their Native Country...shall be slaves. A Negro, mulatto, and Indian slaves...shall be held as real estate."[lxxiv] In this "law", the usual temporary bondage first established became lifelong servitude from which not even children might escape. Virginia's colonial government legally redefined human bondage to change the status of servant to slave and human beings to property with a sweeping legal declaration. Enslaved people were under the force of law deprived of their basic rights and viewed as objects for use as their legal owner decided.

Due to centuries of practiced servitude, even tribal kings in Africa participated in the slave trade and provided fellow Africans to sell abroad. To acquire firearms and several other manufactured goods the African kings used slaves as currency and one educational organization explains most "viewed the people they sold not as fellow Africans but criminals, debtors, or prisoners of war from rival tribes. By selling them kings enriched their own realms and strengthened them against neighboring enemies." "African kingdoms prospered from the slave trade but meeting the Europeans massive demand created intense competition".[lxxv] We can see the deep human need for competition fuel an existing pernicious system and force greater injustices on both sides of the Atlantic.

Similar to the Native American and European dehumanization of outsiders to the rank of slave, the African kings too set aside morality for lucrative trade. African leaders altered tribal law to replace several other normal criminal sentences with slavery and the capture of slaves became not just a consequence of war but a motive for waging it. Those tribes with firearms raided others without them and this drove raided tribes to enslave others to acquire superior foreign weaponry inciting a continental "arms race". This system was prorogated by ruling classes on both sides of the Atlantic Ocean for the benefit of maintaining power and dominance over competing factions. An often-incomplete picture of slavery's past without necessary context forgoes discussion of the shared responsibility multiple cultures bear for its effects on the American continents.

Guided in part by our biological need to dominate those around us the English crown decided upon a drastic inhuman business expansion. "English suppliers responded to the increasing demand for slaves. In 1672, England officially got into the slave trade as the King of England chartered the Royal African Company, encouraging it to expand the British slave trade." The number of Africans brought to the colonies on British vessels increased from five thousand to forty-five thousand per year. This led to England surpassing Portugal and Spain as the number one slave trafficker in the world supplying its colonies in America. This system of domination likely would have continued to expand internationally until growing political unrest in the English colonies became a widespread revolution.

The United States is a young country founded on revolutionary principals seeking to balance the legal rights of the individual with the laws of the government. Many of its founders were a political dichotomy, slave-holding colonial rebels fighting an imperial power to achieve personal freedom. The American Revolution is a bold turning point in world history that revived the ideals of ancient Greek democracy but America was not a nation of just ideals but similar to all other nations was comprised of flawed leaders desiring greater authority. During the first century of America's existence, widely differing regional politics and interests vied to control the growing nation's destiny. Tragically, many leaders in the United States used existing European imperial methods to justify the practice of slavery as legitimate business and rendered human beings into property.

The first great crime the young United States government bore responsibility for is helping perpetuate institutional slavery. The oldest descendants of former slaves still keenly feel the costs and noble stories of humanity were lost in the passage of time. Yet some Native American tribes, several European nations, and all of colonial America held slaves in differing numbers and during 1790, almost three million slaves were held in forced captivity. A growing minority of religious leaders, abolitionist citizens, and free people opposed the system of oppression and eventually many states outlawed the practice. However, roughly half of the United States by the 1800s relied upon institutional slavery to maintain profitable businesses and communities.

As the slave trade continued, other American leaders focused on expanding the territory of the United States without concern to existing cultures in the path of desired expansion. Several past United States public and religious figures endorsed policies to push the boundaries of America to the Pacific Ocean that eventually would be termed "manifest destiny". The doctrine called for the vast assumption of land and the removal of existing native groups living on the desired territory or controlling valuable resources. This continued national drive for expansion led to a deal between French and American officials for the Louisiana Territory and fueled concessions with Britain to acquire the southern Oregon Country. President Andrew Jackson passed the Indian Removal Act of 1830 that led to the infamous Trail of Tears and several tribes did not comply with the new "voluntary" law and resisted forced relocation orders.

Incited officials drove the Native Americans further west in regular intervals before the young nation's expanding population. For many native people relocating became a death march westward because United States officials failed to offer promised supplies for the journey and it resulted in further native mortality from disease and starvation. "Of the 15,000 Creek who marched to their new home in Oklahoma, only 3,500 survived the journey...16,000 Cherokee who were forced to move from several south-eastern states to present day Oklahoma, 4,000 died due to disease, starvation, and adverse weather conditions. In all, tens of thousands of American Indians, some estimates are close to 100,000, lost their lives and their homelands in the series of forced migrations."[lxxvi]

During the 1830s, the Republic of Texas gained independence and public debate about its annexation to the United States led the Mexican government to conduct border attacks. President James Polk publicly endorsed the expansionist doctrine, America annexed Texas, and Polk saw an opportunity when a minor border dispute escalated. This skirmish became the Mexican-American War and resulted in America conquering nearly a third of Mexico before dividing the land into what later constitutes several modern states. Manifest destiny would play a significant influence to justify the primal need for securing natural resources without afterthoughts to the expansive violence and suffering endured by troops and civilians on both sides. This mixture of displacement and war led to the rapid expansion of the United States during successive periods at the cost of the native people who survived repeated European colonizations.

The transition from being a part of the English imperial mixed economy to capitalist free market economics provided an unlikely opponent to slavery and racially motivated class. The modern United States economy functions on capitalism; this economic system relies upon portions of the founding principles of basic mammalian trade and reciprocation. Successful repeated interactions within social creatures using reciprocal trade are verifiable and this engenders the desire to trade again. Traditional economic systems are the ancient type of free barter in which people can set a value to desirable things based on supply and demand including what labor and products are worth to their society. Certain trades were valued more based on environment, fashion, utility, and the acquisition of capital provides a means for garnering status or influence that allowed those denied rank in the abolished English nobility to rise and reduce corruption by rewarding meritorious behavior and skill.

Some might claim all good work is equally valuable but fail to consider the market such good work occurs within; since trade does not occur in a vacuum, external forces necessarily influence value. We can easily understand why boat oars rather than fleece coats would be more popular and valuable to a tropical island nation. No matter how beautiful and well-constructed the heavy coat might be it has no purpose in this particular society and thus demand makes the value of boat oars exceed coats. Free trade does not assign value by good work but useful work, if there is no demand for a product it rightly fails. Humans incorporated these principles into the ideals of voluntary trade and when fair reciprocation occurs, it is the most successful type of human economic interaction.

The free trade system has been the engine of progress for millions of years with gradual refinement into what existing versions still operate. Free trade has broken down the barriers of language, religion, cultural taboos, and discrimination based on the overwhelming desires of human social exploration in the higher mind and the lower brain's greed. We are in part selfish and prone to fulfilling our desires at the expense of others and this in a sense creates the unexpected environment for possible trade benefits outweighing our natural suspicion of others. Repeated successful trade can lead to mutual economic growth when people operate ethically and might secure greater diplomacy or even political alliances. Naturally formed social hierarchies combat unfair trade practices with loss of trade, status, wealth, freedom, and a number of accepted consequences. The vast majority of successful developed countries use a form of economic free trade because it resonates within our biology.

Unfortunately, some modern groups violently demand their version of "equity" instead of legal equality no matter how unfair or impossible such demands might prove. Recent "equity" proponents desire the exact same outcome for all people and deem any differences in reward to present institutional bias. Such ideas neglect to consider all personal choice and variances in experience and this kind of "equity" reduces all human accomplishment to the same mediocrity. It offers no reason for people to excel when they expect an equal reward for less achievement and under this system, anyone desiring the paycheck but forgoing the effort thrives equally with hard working people. Conversely, the current system of equality of opportunity allows everyone a chance to succeed based upon his or her own merit and efforts.

Another key component of America's economic success is support from democratic republicanism; a political system founded upon democratic voting paired with elected representatives in the form of a republic. A key facet of the American system is the division of powers that prevents too much centralized power in the hands of too few people. The use of an electoral college further checks the will of the people with political appointees to prevent mob rule or domination of the country by popular tyrants. Despite these protections, the separation of powers in the American constitution, and the beneficial properties of capitalism there are still obvious problems.

The flaws of unregulated capitalism include corruption and the system has and can go wrong in varying American business and institutional sectors. Corporate fraud, toothless regulation, and corporate socialism reside among the most corrupt practices of modern government. In the past industrial robber barons held business monopolies in the United States that allowed too much unregulated growth and commanded unfair influence. Yet eventually the United States government broke these huge entities into smaller corporations to provide the overall system more legal equality because effective regulation is essential to promote a successful and fair economic system. Thus, it is necessary to prevent corporations from unethically amassing too much control within the financial or social hierarchy.

All these possible negative influences do not invalidate the economic system, the beneficial gains still occur but when the system grows unfair in portions it needs gradual adjustment to properly reflect ethical trade standards. Regulators should hold corporations to the same account as citizens, when they fail, they should lose everything just like a citizen does. They have assumed the free speech rights of citizens under corporate personhood and should not possess a safety net that citizens lack themselves. Being a "person" should include all the legal disadvantages and the healthy regulation of companies is necessary to prevent corruption or market interference that breeds unethical financial disparity.

The critics of capitalism often point out that it can lead to vast differences in wealth, but this is not resulting from some mystical intrinsic evil in free markets. Not every part of the disparity equation is from negative influences and subject to many factors beyond simplistic criticisms. One vital consideration is work; how much work is a person willing to do? Shall they deny themselves decades of comfort and time with friends and family; will they not have children to achieve their ambitions? Can they accept a stressful life of constant activity for possible success? A fair system rewards a person based on the merits of their labor and sacrifices with consideration to the supply and demand of the market.

Most people shall not make the significant investments of time or sacrifice to achieve their maximum productivity. Those who do by the very nature of their sacrifices deserve more in return if they succeed, they are more productive, they contribute more to the society, and without a class of driven workers a society flounders into disrepair. It does not matter if the job is a bricklayer or a nuclear scientist; the hardest working people deserve more for their labors than someone not ambitious or driven receives. To reward mediocrity and merit equally is to reduce all standards eventually to an equally lowest common denominator. Not all jobs should pay the same because of differing educational costs, technical experience, and innovations that deserve greater reward on the overall scale of achievement. Jobs with significant challenges and potentially lethal environmental dangers by the nature of their greater potential costs should have commensurate benefits. The most qualified and hardworking person deserves to make the most, not only is this fair but also drives the ambitions of others to achieve.

The United States constitution provides for equality under the law and offers a nation where all may pursue reasonable happiness but no legal assurance should exist. Legal equality and the most level playing field possible is essential but farcical ideas to assure equal outcomes for all people ignores the endless variations in human behavior and environment. The utopian desires of various groups do not translate into reality and forgo understanding the nature of human beings, economics, and the desire for self-determination. Most people do not wish to surrender their will to a government or economic system relying on principles in utter opposition to humanity's most elemental patterns of behavior.

In less than a century, the American political system guided by free market progress created a rapid expansion of industrialization. The northern United States economic boom expanded trade and business interests that outpaced the southern economy based on slavery. Machines began to replace workers, innovation and competition could produce greater amounts of products with less capital investment that did not rely solely on forced labor. The southern United States required involuntary labor that placed increasing unachievable demands on a largely static population for expansion and it began to weaken under the weight of unchecked corruption, resource demands, and repeated public dissent.

In 1860, slave populations reduce to just over 361,000 people from expanding abolitionist efforts, changing public opinion, and state laws coupled with technological innovation or industrial expansion.[lxxvii] A growing conflict between North and South on the horizon would develop into a huge death count comprised entirely of Americans. Slavery's abolition occurred in less than a century following the American Revolution at the cost of hundreds of thousands of lives and billions of dollars in the United States Civil War. In the aftermath of the war, slaves became American citizens and the United States lost a President to a Confederate assassin. While America did not begin or propagate the infernal practice as some people claim, there is no excuse for the nearly a century the practice was allowed to continue. Yet history exacted a dire price for aiding this unfathomable attack on human rights in a land that prides itself on defending freedom.

The monumental cost of slavery in lives and suffering by carrying on past injustices required multiple great and necessary sacrifices made by later generations to destroy this same practice.

Slavery nearly split the United States asunder and remains a charged historical matter because it challenges our basic humanity and forces us to confront the crimes of the past. However, no living person is responsible for this great injustice and the only way to render some modern clarity is to learn the real facts of this ancient plague on humankind. "Plantation slavery in the antebellum South rightfully looms large in history, but ignoring other forms of bondage in the American past narrows our scope of understanding and makes it difficult to engage in broader global debates about diverse-and ongoing- practices of slavery, servitude, and other forms of existing captivity."[lxxviii] If we ignore the facts of the matter, we can never understand this is not just a cultural but human pattern.

The results of the American Civil War incited existing racism and led some white citizens to attribute postwar financial losses singularly to slavery's abolition instead of the expansive military defeat. Southern anger at black citizens using their legal rights inspired barbaric attempts to create widespread terror and the perpetrators of illegal collective violence attempted to justify their actions using Jim Crow style laws. Despite the legal methods to oppress former slaves being undertaken, it still was not enough for the murderous among the ranks of the hateful. According to the National Association for the Advancement of Colored People, a detestable form of local murderous aggression continued for another century in some parts of the United States.

The gruesome practice of lynching began during the nineteenth century to extended past the middle of the twentieth and from "1882-1968, 4, 743 lynchings occurred in the United States. Of these people, 3,446 were black. The blacks lynched accounted for 72.7% of the people lynched" the remainder of people killed are white people who tried to aid blacks, opposed lynching, or were guilty of domestic crimes. These statistics verify the real lethal threat of racism prior to civil rights protections and the dysfunction of the legal system in portions of the country. "Most of the lynching that took place happened in the South. A big reason for this was the end of the Civil War."[lxxix] The practice of vigilante murders is unjustifiable and those who practiced it should have been provided the same fate as their victims under the mantle of law and been forever marked by their deeds. The study of historic tragedy and injustice is not just for the most outspoken advocate but also for the citizen who desires to know all the facts about a nation. While lynching was not a coordinated effort by the American government, some individual local officials certainly participated and were aware of this rampant injustice.

Racial oppression would rear its ugly head internationally during the twentieth century on multiple occasions and the United States aided in the destruction of such tyrannical regimes for ideological and political reasons. For a time, America tried to follow the advice of its founders and not become embroiled in foreign wars but a few legitimate threats provided greater reasoning for ambitious leaders to increasingly view war as the natural extension of policy when diplomacy failed. Many underestimated the countless resources and human costs required to undertake a series of expanding foreign operations and military engagements. Such wars proved exceedingly deadly not just for American soldiers but foreign civilians as well.

From 1900 until 1990, less than one million American soldiers died in every war combined during that period and we might contrast this against thirty-four million civilians killed during WWII alone. Civilians are "shot, bombed, raped, starved, and driven from their homes and during World War II, 135,000 civilians died in two days in the firebombing of Dresden." While America's efforts supporting the Allies in WWII were essential to the maintenance of a free societies and stopping the genocide of several groups by the Nazis, these efforts undertook expansive violence against German civilians. Operation Thunderclap was the code name for the Allied military actions focused against the German city of Dresden that some claim was not a strategic target supplying the Nazi war machine whose destruction provided no appreciable wartime benefit.

Conversely, modern declassified files note British Air Marshal Charles Portal's military strategy to demoralize the German population and war effort by "indiscriminate 'area bombing' by night of all German cities with populations exceeding 100,000." Thus, despite the claims that Dresden had no value English leaders had set military parameters which transformed the city into a target. Military interest however does not detract from the horrors observed by groups attempting to clean up Dresden; one group seeking possible survivors that took shelter underground would find no corpses. All that remained were bones sticking out of a vile liquid comprised of melted civilian bodies who sought escape from nights of falling incendiary weapons.

Many who could not escape underground littered the streets burnt and shriveled to almost half their normal height with the youngest victims reportedly vaporized.[lxxx] A week later, in Pforzheim, Germany, 17,800 people were killed in 22 minutes."[lxxxi] When our actions feel justified any sort of mass devastation might occur guided by primal disgust and fear mechanisms to satisfy collective aggression. While the crimes of the Nazis were almost limitless, the disgust of some Allied commanders forming policy turned upon German civilian populations. The citizens of every nation bombed during the war were dehumanized to become statistical targets and not living people, their death was more valuable to the war effort than any living contributions.

Naturally, the arms race to win increasingly grew more frantic as nations raced to construct a dominant weapon and this resulted in the greatest engine of destruction ever devised by humanity, the atomic bomb. In Nazi Germany, the increasingly unjust detention and murder of Jewish citizens forced talented scientists to escape and many immigrated to the United States during 1939. Within the refugee population were scientists Albert Einstein and Enrico Fermi who contacted the United States government bearing a warning about the recent success Axis powers had splitting a uranium atom. Fear of the Axis powers developing a bomb that would destroy enemy cities or forces en masse inspired President Franklin D. Roosevelt to approve a budget and staff for atomic research.

Following the Japanese attack on Pearl Harbor, the atomic group fell under the jurisdiction of the United States War Department and this would introduce greater military controls over the project. During the same period, Japanese Americans would suffer due to political hysteria at home and Roosevelt would institute unjust legal demands upon the civilian population. Perhaps the greatest American government single mass violation of citizen rights in the twentieth century was the internment of Japanese adults and children in prison camps during World War II. President Franklin D. Roosevelt used public fear and disgust to present an executive order forcing greater than one hundred thousand people to relocate into military style detention camps in the wake of destruction at Pearl Harbor. Roosevelt sought to prevent espionage without a policy selectively targeting legitimate threats and instead ordered mass imprisonment of any person with biological similarity to enemy forces.

A resulting public outcry for these civil rights violations included advocates that included future president Dwight D. Eisenhower publicly offering the camps held several innocent people. Roosevelt's order additionally inspired a chain of other countries to expel Japanese citizens among their populations as well in support of the United States. The internment of Japanese Americans reveals the oppressive potential of unchecked government power to secure national security policies and such action is not limited to political party or social ideology because all people are capable of allowing irrationality to guide them. Subsequently officials used devastating atomic weapons on the Japanese cities of Nagasaki and Hiroshima with deaths totals exceeding a hundred thousand people within moments. Less immediately catastrophic but more sustained methods were used against Tokyo during the same war and two atomic bombs could not rival the eventual death toll firebombing would inflict upon the Japanese capital. From the ashes of war, most countries were in shambles or defeated beyond most chances of launching effective future resistance.

The greatest two players upon the world stage in the period following World War II were the United States and Soviet Union. America was at times in the last century regarded by several in the West as the lead bastion of freedom and Russia was its repressive Communist nemesis. America internationally championed democratic governments but some of its leaders decided to engage in clandestine undemocratic policies. Politics, tribalism, and the usual negative traits of humans led American leaders eventually to undertake illegal operations using national security justifications. One battleground against the chosen enemies of democracy was amid the transforming landscape of postwar China.

To secure American interests the Office of Strategic Services, a military intelligence predecessor group to the Central Intelligence Agency, supported anti-Communist General Chiang Kai-shek's bid to control China. Circumstances prior necessitated the Chinese nationalist military to collaborate with communist forces against the Japanese, and the United States following the war provided support troops to aid only Kai-shek's forces. American soldiers helping to seize and hold areas of the country in opposition to the communist leadership of Mao Tse-tung and Chou En-lai further incited the ongoing Chinese civil war. According to one account, roughly one hundred thousand United States troops were present in China during 1946 aiding Kai-shek under the pretense of disarming and repatriating Japanese prisoners.

Subsequently the United States undertook troop withdrawals but reportedly poured billions of dollars in aid to the nationalist forces against the ascending communist movement. Despite these expansive attempts to support nationalist forces, General Chiang's brutal actions paired with the corruption of the regime destroyed his ability to control the Chinese cities. Communist forces overwhelmed mainland China and this caused all nationalist forces to retreat and regroup on the island of Taiwan. It appeared that some American leaders could not accept the Chinese selection of communism over democracy and continued providing assistance to Chang Kai-shek's forces. Years of repeated violent paramilitary campaigns targeting Chinese Communists may explain some of the modern animosity between the two nations.[lxxxii]

America soon realized that Joseph Stalin was not the ally it had expected but a tyrant ruling over his people with a steel fist. Following the descent of the Iron Curtain, Russia became the seat of power to a Communist empire with openly repressive policies including the widespread use of murder domestically. American leaders chose plots and coups to counter Soviet postwar domination of clandestine techniques despite the foreseeable long-term consequences to America's reputation. Because they used morally unjustified means outside of lawful combat, it compromises the usual evocation of fighting a threat to serve the cause of freedom. This inconsistency was not lost on the Soviet Union or its propaganda machine.

The Cold War quickly developed in Korea as Russia and the United States occupied portions of the nation to expel the Japanese and reunite the country. Dr. Russell Jack Smith, a former CIA Deputy Director of Intelligence commented on the futility of trying to impose democracy on Korea from his direct involvement in the matter. "Korea had been a unified country for centuries until its division in 1945 into Chinese and America zones. Now, a scant eight years later and immediately after a devastating three-year war, which had wrought great damage...we were asking for high standards of democratic government. It seems now that we almost took it for granted that the millions of Koreans living south of the thirty-eight parallel would enter joyously into the creation of a semi-Korea, a half Korea called South Korea and would reject the northern half their ancestors had ruled and freely moved about in."[lxxxiii]

However, neither emerging superpower's plans would allow them to cede areas of control to the opposing ideology's forces. This would lead to escalating border clashes at the thirty-eighth parallel and calls for their enemy's annihilation to unite the Korean peninsula. The Korean War was a proxy battle with the United States aiding South Korea against North Korea that collaborated with Russia and China. The war sundered Korea, killed two million of its people, and over thirty thousand Americans died in the fighting. Officials never formally ended the war via a peace treaty and nearly seven decades later the country remains split due to the ideological differences of the last century and there is no clear sign any reunification is forthcoming.

As the Cold War expanded, a fearful hysteria began to grip the United States with the rise of McCarthyism based on a handful of legitimate spies but more on the implication of rampant spy rings and endless Communist domestic betrayers. The human need to seek patterns influenced by fear can render normal personal interactions to guilt by association. Some American political and intelligence leaders reinforced this linkage and it resulted in a political witch-hunt leading to public attacks upon many communist's relatives, friends, or associates. Yet this was just a single threat and not the only psychologically inspired danger targeting American or foreign citizens based upon official fears run amok.

One example of the CIA's later attempts to control the mental and social behaviors of humans with drugs and hypnosis was codenamed Project ARTICHOKE. This project was an extension of earlier programs named MKULTRA designed to influence the mind and behavior of its targets. Bulgarian expatriate Dimitur Adamov Dimitrov was an anti-Fascist fighter during 1943 but the next year he journeyed to multiple areas while advocating for local populations to fight against Communist activities. It seems his Bulgarian nationalist liberation group was more committed to Bulgarian independence from the Soviets than left-or right-wing ideals. Following his later capture by Communist forces, he escaped to Greece and joined other like-minded people that established a political group. He was according to one report working for Radio Athens during the 1940s to broadcast pro-Western propaganda efforts against the Soviet Union.

During 1951, Agency Deputy Director for Plans Frank G. Wisner granted Dimitrov Provisional Operation Clearance for ninety days as a contract agent for use in political, psychological, and guerilla warfare operations under Project QKSTAIR. He according to one file was "...utilized by OPC in Athens, Greece and provided 21 agents for infiltration into Bulgaria." Just two months later Dimitrov's antisocial manner quickly irked others in the project and officials became suspicious that he was misappropriating funds. They were additionally concerned that he met with a French military attaché because he might reveal his knowledge of Agency operations. A related document using Dimitrov's pseudonym reveals that he "...has been warned repeatedly to maintain as good security as possible regarding his purpose for which he has rented offices...Nevertheless, (Dimitrov) has blabbed his business (and ours!) all over Athens" and one commenting official suggests he might be mentally unstable. This claim may have inspired using Dimitrov to observe the effects of extended isolation and incarceration with limited human contact.

Discussions between military officials and Agency leaders at the CIA Athens Station led to plans for having Dimitrov detained in a hospital and the visit of a French military officer to Dimitrov in April of 1951 further spurred intelligence leaders to act. Dimitrov's supposed friend Yani Kolomonos told a CIA source that Dimitrov sought to "give the French detailed accounts of all United States operations of which he is aware" for a cash payment. "Kolomonos suggested that this effort of the French might be a communist inspired attempt to penetrate United States intelligence activities." However, imprisonment was not their lone option they pondered considering the "disposal of Dimitrov since he had full knowledge of names of next infiltration teams and general knowledge of operations." A second official account termed his knowledge of operations limited but "it was considered extremely undesirable to allow these facts into French hands. Arrangements were therefore made with Greek authorities for his arrest just before his scheduled meeting with the French representative".[lxxxiv] [lxxxv]

Greek authorities held Dimitrov until American officials sent him to a hospital in Germany and conducted mental observation for multiple days. Agency operatives later held Dimitrov in a Panamanian mental hospital despite that he was sane for three years and considered attempting to use drugs to remove parts of his memory but opted for illegal extended incarceration. CIA officials decided following a debriefing in nineteen fifty-three that "whatever operational knowledge he had was obsolete" and they release Dimitrov to Greece then subsequently fail to secure his migration to "Canada, New Zealand, Australia, and elsewhere". Ultimately, their plan to conceal Dimitrov failed when he immigrated to the United States and became "a continual source of embarrassment".

Dimitrov began a letter writing campaign to several prominent United States officials including President's Richard Nixon, Dwight Eisenhower, and John F. Kennedy to request political appointments. Dimitrov further sought to schedule meetings with Richard Nixon in 1960 and later CIA Director Allen Dulles while claiming on multiple occasions of being able to liberate the Balkan countries under Soviet rule with time and government financial assistance. Agency contacts reported much official consternation that Dimitrov attempted to sell a political film to the Department of State and he approached the United States Embassy in Greece representing himself as the leader of a Bulgarian Liberation movement. Calling himself General Dico Dimitrov, he received awards and media publicity for his advocacy of the Vietnam War and France. Officials determined that despite the prior excessive demeanor and the single allegation of mental instability that he was in fact sane. By the end of all their efforts, the Agency had only succeeded in embarrassing itself to suppress a man they never should have used in the first place.

Assassinations and Nation Building

In early 1950s, the young Central Intelligence Agency had immense goals but lacked the power to achieve them and it would not take long for intelligence leaders to attempt bold action to establish the Agency's significance within international affairs. At this time, multiple nations established policies to destabilize enemy governments and one example is among the efforts by the United States on behalf of its Cold War ally England. The leaders of Iran had prior allied with the Axis Powers during WWII, supported Jewish persecution, and later business interests provided an excuse for revenge. A Central Intelligence Agency history explains that in 1952 the Iranian government led by democratically elected Premier Mohammed Mossadeq would not reach an oil settlement with "interested Western countries". Iran's government attempted to nationalize the oil supply, seize foreign corporate holdings, and break the influence of powerful Western corporations over its national resources. Spurred by calls for assistance from their English Secret Intelligence Service (SIS, MI6) counterparts the Agency forecast that if Mossadeq retained power, there would be dire consequences. During 1953, Mossadeq was cooperating with fellow Iranian political groups including local communists and the unlikely possibility Iran would fall behind the Iron Curtain served as the justification for covert action.

The express purpose of Agency Project TPAJAX was "to cause the fall of the Mossadeq government; to reestablish the prestige and power of the Shah; and to replace the Mossadeq government with one which would govern Iran according to constructive policies".[lxxxvi] Regardless of intentions, the policy was anything but constructive and violated the sovereignty of the Iranian nation, replaced Mossadeq with a foreign pawn, and eventually set up a reign of terror by the SAVAK police under the Shah. Iran suffered huge political, religious, and economic unrest that still lingers today and the CIA has borne most blame for an SIS inspired operation that was jointly undertaken. Despite repeated claims of the United States being alone responsible for the unlawful overthrow, England called upon the Americans for aid to wrest control of Iran from its rightful leadership.

The next year a similar occurrence transpired in the South American nation of Guatemala against the elected government of Jacobo Arbenz. Even with the prior collaboration between Arbenz and the United States government, the President of Guatemala attempted land reforms that targeted international corporate properties and created dissent in the local military. A clandestine government overthrow plan was given the codename PBSUCCESS and during 1954 a military junta with CIA resources and weapons supported by a naval blockade displaced the Guatemalan government. A junta leader who reversed the land reforms and targeted former officials with imprisonment and death replaced Arbenz. Strikingly the project's related documents included a guide to assassinating people with a list of potential targets of value.

"A Study of Assassination" is the Central Intelligence Agency document authored in 1954 that provided suggestions for the best methods to exterminating a human target. It further included tips for avoiding discovery, proper weapon usage, and establishing cover stories to conceal guilt. The guide includes warnings to those intelligence officials who consider using such techniques "Murder is not morally justifiable...Persons who are morally squeamish should not attempt it...Assassination is an extreme measure not normally used in clandestine operations. It should be assumed it will never be ordered or authorized by any U.S. Headquarters, though the latter may in rare instances agree to its execution by members of an associated foreign service." Thus, while first stating no moral and lawful authority would order assassination, the Agency official quickly created an exception for this by using outside assistance. Such a vague commitment to the legitimate purpose of intelligence operations and the willingness of some leaders to undermine prescribed conduct is revealing. When someone asserts no democratically elected official would plot murders for political gain, history often disagrees.

The study recommends if assassination is the chosen method it must "be confined to an absolute minimum of persons. Ideally, only one person will be involved." Public claims that intelligence services always use large groups in assassination plots are improbable because it defeats the very nature of keeping a secret. The study prefers labeling a lone individual responsible for the project in the case of discovery to absorb deserved operational blowback. Another consideration is different procedures for killing targets and whether the assassin shall escape or it requires their death. Desirable traits for assassins included courage, resourcefulness, intelligence, great physical health, and convenient expendability or concealment following the crime.

"The specific technique employed will depend upon a large number of variables, but should be constant in one point: Death must be absolutely certain. The attempt on Hitler's life failed because the conspiracy did not give the matter proper attention." Vital to any successful plot is the use of exacting force to assure no chance of a target's survival, and if necessary, the assassin will join them in eternity. If the plot called for the assassin to die the candidate should be a "fanatic of some sort", "handled with extreme care", and the handling agent will "conduct any withdrawal or covering action which may be necessary."[lxxxvii] The assassin is just another piece on the game board of clandestine intelligence and thus expendable because a successful assassination requires insulating the conspirators.

Another factor in the assassination equation is determining the proper environment and means for maximizing the chances of success. To best utilize the tools available in their environment the killer must possess some anatomical knowledge of humans. Intelligence officials do not recommend murdering a person with your bare hands (strangulation or beating) due to the skill level necessary for a quick and traceless death. "A hammer, axe, wrench, screw driver, fire poker, kitchen knife, lamp stand, or anything hard, heavy and handy will suffice. A length of rope or wire or a belt will do if the assassin is strong or agile. All such improvised weapons have the important advantage of availability and apparent innocence." Should the assassin not be able to obtain a weapon they can use their environment for lethal results while maintaining little obvious suspicion.

The document advises one can stage accidents if the target suffers a fall of at least "75 feet or more onto a hard surface. Elevator shafts, stairwells, unscreened windows and bridges will serve. Bridge falls into water are not reliable. In simple cases a private meeting with the subject may be arranged at a properly-cased location. This act may be executed by sudden, vigorous [excised] of the ankles, tipping the subject over the edge. If the assassin immediately sets up an outcry, playing the 'horrified witness' no alibi or surreptitious withdrawal is necessary. In chase cases it will usually be necessary to stun or drug the subject before dropping him. Care is required to ensure that no wound or condition not attributable to the fall is discernible after death. Falls into the sea or swiftly flowing rivers may suffice if the subject cannot swim. It will be more reliable if the assassin can arrange to attempt rescue, as he can thus be sure of the subject's death and at the same time establish a workable alibi."[lxxxviii]

Other conceived "accidents" included fabricated circumstances to explain unlikely details leading to a target's death. Victims can be pushed into oncoming "...trains or subway cars...but require exact timing and can seldom be free from unexpected observation." Agency officials do not recommend using car accidents because if "the subject is deliberately run down, very exact timing is necessary and investigation is likely to be thorough. If the subject's car is tampered with, reliability is very low." They instead suggest stunning or drugging the subject, placing them in a car, and dropping it off "a high cliff or into deep water without observation."

Alcohol or drugs might prepare someone for a "contrived accident of any kind" based upon the specific habits of the target. "If the subject drinks heavily, morphine or a similar narcotic can be injected at the passing out stage, and the cause of death will often be held to be acute alcoholism. Specific poisons, such as arsenic or strychnine, are effective but their possession or procurement is incriminating, and accurate dosage is problematical." Depending on diseases or physical addictions of the victim, a suitable tool can be selected for effectiveness paired with subtlety because while death was of primary importance, the ability to kill someone and vanish is highly valued.

If the situation precludes accidents then using direct action with various weapons is a possibility. Using edged weapons (knives, machetes, hatchets) with proper knowledge of the best striking locations on the victim can prove effective. "Puncture wound of the body cavity may not be reliable unless the heart is reached. The heart is protected by the rib cage and is not always easy to locate." The study remarks that a reduction in prior mortal abdominal wounds due to advances in medical treatment likely renders such methods unadvisable. The guide notes complete assurance of death using edged weapons requires "severing the spinal cord...This can be done with the point of a knife or a light blow of an axe or hatchet." Blunt weapons required similar knowledge of the human body and strikes must "be directed to the temple, the area just below and behind the ear, and the lower, rear portion of the skull. Of course, if the blow is very heavy, any portion of the upper skull will do."

Firearms were the most often utilized weapon for political assassinations in the last century because few weapons can offer reliability and permit attacking from a distance. They range from small caliber handguns to powerful rifles and each has a proper circumstance and success rate that can be drastically affected by the environment or utilizing assassin. "The precision rifle...a good hunting or target rifle should always be considered as a possibility...Public figures or guarded officials may be killed with great reliability and some safety if a firing point can be established prior to an official occasion." Conversely, the guide states despite the frequent use of firearms they often are misused because of inexperience and rifles too can be difficult to conceal. The study recommends machine guns in some instances facing guarded targets with established visibility, submachine guns can be "useful in assassination" but they are less powerful and require closer placement near the target rendering them less safe. Shotguns are powerful short-range weapons yet suffer an even greater distance safety problem than submachine guns and require the user to be just out the victim's reach. Pistols can be useful and provide easy concealment but unless the weapon is high caliber and operated by a proficient user, they fail to kill targets nearly as often as they succeed.

Explosives have "been used frequently in assassination", these weapons allow the assassin to maintain distance and this provides greater security to a plot. "The charge must be very large and the detonation must be controlled exactly as to time by the assassin who can observe the subject." The study recommends against using smaller bombs and improvised traps due to unreliability and may result in unintended deaths that might create "public reactions unfavorable to the cause for which the assassination is carried out." It reminds no "assassination instruction should ever be written or recorded" and this is a supreme irony due to the study's existence.

"A Study of Assassination" provided a general outline for clandestine murder at the behest of those destabilizing enemy foreign governments and included how, when, and where to kill a target. The actual reason why is not always so clear since officials later provided some of these methods to paramilitary groups and this allowed dangerous methods to spread among non-official groups without any operational limitations and once those secrets escaped, no amount of attempting to suppress the effect would succeed. United States intelligence groups with the approval of later governments continued a policy of intervention in foreign nations with often-disastrous results for local populations and future diplomacy. The study is a reminder that powerful groups contriving plans to annihilate enemies in the pursuit of advantage and hide all traces is a historically repeating cycle.

United States President Dwight Eisenhower was a West Point trained cold warrior that served as Supreme Commander of North Atlantic Treaty Organization (NATO) and later as the President of Columbia University. However, Eisenhower's liberal education did not blunt his distaste for communism and desire to stamp out the Red Menace by any means necessary. Eisenhower and several other leading World War II commanders likely felt a deep betrayal with the fall of the Iron Curtain and Stalin's reversal from ally to disdainful tyrant. Following the French colonial withdrawal from Vietnam and its loss to Communist forces, the United States provided military advisers during 1954 to the recently formed southern Republic of Vietnam.

The French surrogate Emperor Bao Dai controlled the nation until rabid anti-Communist Ngo Dihn Diem gained power with support from the United States and eventually launched a wide campaign against communism. Diem in this period would target rival nationalist factions as well that did not support his rise to power and inadvertently filled the ranks of the Viet Cong with disenfranchised citizens. "Presidential ordinances enacted by Diem in early 1956 permitted local officials to imprison, interrogate, and execute suspected communists or communist sympathizers outside of the judicial system." "Thousands of Vietnamese were imprisoned and tortured for years without trial. Corrupt local officials often exploited the ordinances for various reasons aimed at personal gain" which led to non-communists being targeted and turned public opinion against the government inquisition. The Diem regime killed entire generations of villagers and political opponents and this inspired a brutal campaign of retribution by opposition forces.

Because of the counterattacks, the United States escalated military operations amid "the growing level of discontent" and Diem labeled southern Communists and their sympathizers as "Viet Cong". The Communists retaliated by "assassinating local government officials by the hundreds" and in 1959 the North Vietnam Communist government backed dissident agents in the south to enacting widespread political subversion operations and armed group ambushes. lxxxix The violence and terror Diem inflicted upon others would subsequently target him, but prior to his reckoning American officials deemed another world leader a national security threat.

Republic of the Congo Prime Minster Patrice Lumumba concerned the Eisenhower administration due to Lumumba's meetings and diplomacy with Soviet interests. The Congo was a source of vital uranium for American national security purposes and when Lumumba contacted the Soviets for aid, it became possible this access would be lost. Thus in 1960, United States leaders tasked the Central Intelligence Agency with eliminating Lumumba by political assassination and began to assess possible assassin candidates. Agency chemist and biological weapons expert Sidney Gottlieb played a significant role in disseminating the orders to kill Lumumba and providing the necessary means. Gottlieb met with Larry Devlin the Chief of Station in Leopoldville at his apartment to inform him that "lethal biological agents had been developed for the assassination of Lumumba...The poisonous substances were to be injected in to food, drink, toothpaste, or anything else Lumumba might ingest."xc

Simultaneously, CIA officer William K. Harvey was hiring spotters and potential assassins to use against Lumumba and other potential future targets. However, unfolding events would render the poison or assassins unnecessary when a United States official incited the Congolese opposition forces. CIA Station Chief Devlin told a ranking Congolese military officer Lumumba planned to seize power and this led military forces to overthrow and later execute the Prime Minster. The ranking Congolese officer became the new military dictator Mobutu Sese Seko that served American interests and led a destructive regime in the

Congo for decades resulting from this pivotal but unproven allegation. Lumumba and Mossaddegh's governments were displaced in part by the intelligence operations and officials of the American government. However, not all enemy leaders would prove within the ability of American intelligence to disrupt and proved far more able to damage American security interests.

A year prior Communist revolutionary Fidel Castro secured the Premiership of Cuba, subsequently allied with the Soviet Union, and began to aid revolutionary movements across Latin America. The highest levels of the United States government decided this Communist expansion necessitated Castro's assassination because they would not tolerate a military danger roughly one hundred miles from United States territory. Castro's regime was a legitimate threat but instead of seeking to merely contain him and engage in diplomatic maneuvering, American leaders sought to kill him and likely did not imagine the over half a century of coming blowback. This rising escalation would take humanity to the brink of a nuclear engagement and force a standoff between the superpowers.

American government files affirm, "During the period March 1960 and extending through June 1965, the Agency engaged in a series of schemes to bring about the death or incapacitation of Fidel Castro." Officials contrived using poison cigars, lining his shoes with thallium salts, and planting exploding conch shells before Castro indulged in diving or giving him a scuba suit lined with biological agents. They pondered contaminating the air over a radio station where he spoke, tainting his food or drink, and even a pen that could inject Castro with poison as he signed an official decree. The ideas, funding, and means were limitless but a substantial plan not compromised by the very people it depended on never materialized.

It was during the first phase of operations that American intelligence leaders decided to contact the Italian Mafia; officials believed they could utilize the criminal network to assist them because Castro had seized their vast property and business holdings in Cuba. Yet government leaders failed to understand the Mafioso summoned and believed they might convince the gangsters to send in a pack of sacrificial thugs to murder Castro. The Mafia had other plans that would in time cause officials to provide them blackmail material used to spare one of the criminal leaders from legal charges. Officials attempted to sever all ties, issued denials, and behaved as if the meetings never occurred when government leaders realized the Mafia had been using these meetings to secure future advantage for themselves.

Such miscalculations lead to perhaps the most well-known failed overthrow attempt the Bay of Pigs debacle and officials further militarized the plots in the wake of this failure. The Agency's leaders redoubled their efforts by designing several attack style assassination plans to utilize snipers, explosives, and develop a military overthrow capability. Continued incursions nearly caused atomic war as Soviet countermeasures triggered the Cuban Missile Crisis but those managing intelligence were undeterred and funded dozens of Cuban exile groups. Agency foreign agents undertook operations to launch sabotage, intelligence gathering, and paramilitary raids but this scattershot approach coupled with a misplaced faith in some officials resulted in a series of abandoned, inadvisable, or failed plots.[xci] The Cuban Premier managed to escape the clutches American intelligence based on several factors but vital to ensuring his survival was the role of allied counterintelligence organizations like the Cuban DGI (General Directorate of Intelligence) and Soviet KGB (Committee for State Security). Fidel Castro impressively outlived nearly every person and official from several nations who marked him for death over fifty years prior and reportedly succumbed to natural causes.

While the anti-Castro operations progressed, a formerly classified summary details another United States government connected overthrow, "Rafael Trujillo, the Dominican dictator, was assassinated by Dominican dissidents on the night of 30 May 1961. Although the Agency was involved in supporting those planning the overthrow of Trujillo, as a part of authorized government policy, the actual assassination was a local affair." The CIA attempts to distinguish between training or arming assassins and actually pulling the trigger but even this role establishes their complicity in the act. Trujillo unlike some other targets was a brutal dictator feasibly worthy of overthrowing but the Agency collaboration in supporting his later assassination was a violation of international law and led to subsequent public exposure. The supporters for additional operations did not fully appreciate the eventual far-reaching consequences these interventions would initiate.

Not just obvious intervention but mixed signals and inaction too could render the overthrow of world governments if their allies failed to protect them. Such was the case in the overthrow and murder of the prior mentioned South Vietnam President Ngo Din Diem and his brother Ngo Dihn Nhu following the declaration of martial law in South Vietnam. Both men were corrupt, ambitious, and did not hesitate to use violence against protesting Buddhist populations as the political situation in Vietnam further deteriorated during 1963. The erratic overreach of the Diem brothers made United States officials nervous and opposing policies sparred within internal meetings regarding them. Events culminated in many officials abandoning the Diem brothers and in a few cases actively supporting those who plotted the resulting coup.

One account offered in a related document states "The crucial act, with its overtones of Greek tragedy, opened with a cable. It was dispatched to Saigon late in the evening of August 24, 1963, a date made more significant because it was a Saturday. Washington usually empties on summer weekends...The telegram contained spectacular new instructions for the U.S. embassy in Saigon. It was drawn up at a meeting called by Under-secretary of State Averell Harriman and Roger Hilsman, Assistant Secretary of State for Far Eastern affairs and head of the Vietnam task force. The President's senior advisers were, for the most part, out of town. CIA Director John McCone was in California. Defense Secretary Robert McNamara was on vacation. Secretary of State Dean Rusk was attending a baseball game in New York. President Kennedy was in Hyannis Port. General Taylor says he knew nothing of the meeting until it was over and the telegram long on its way."

This largely unknown message would become a pivotal turning point because it "gave the signal to 'unleash' the Vietnamese military, flashed a green light for the coup against Diem of which the generals had been talking for so many years. The substance of the cable was that U. S. embassy was to make an effort to persuade Diem to fire his brother, release the Buddhist rebels, end press censorship, and restore other democratic liberties suspended under martial law. And if, as the cable anticipated, Diem would not do these things, then the embassy was to contact the Vietnamese generals and tell them that the United States would no longer stand in the way of a revolt."[xcii] While President Diem was quite aware of rumors and signs of his possible displacement, he unlike American leaders was not in repeated contact with specific plotting generals. The CIA was in contact with the generals, the State Department sent opposing commands to the plotting generals followed by cryptic explanations to higher officials upon whose authority they hastily acted. The military conspirators executed Diem and his brother and replaced them with opposition led forces and this act would lead to future oppressive leadership.

Amid the rampant brutality and series of corrupt governments, hopes for success in Vietnam became nearly impossible. Leading United States officials sought to justify continued involvement in a humanitarian catastrophe to fight Communism. Military commanders ignored the ability of troops to resist killing indiscriminately after years of ceaseless war, communist infiltration, and increasingly violent government policies that left many considering all Vietnamese possible enemy collaborators. This increased the likelihood of greater barbarism and later inhumane American war atrocities would serve to bolster copious Communist propaganda.

The My Lai massacre transpired on March 16, 1968 in the Quang Ngai province. United States troops from Charlie Company of the Americal Division's 11th Infantry Brigade had orders to treat all encountered as Viet Cong in the area under the direction of Lieutenant William Calley. Some of the most effective Communist forces were reportedly in nearby combat zones and morale was low in the wake of losses from the Tet Offensive. A mine had just days before injured twenty men and killed one man in their ranks inciting greater shared contempt among the company for local populations. Charlie Company additionally had lost nearly thirty men fighting enemy forces and just more than one hundred men remained alive. The soldiers did not encounter the deadly enemies they expected but found a village known as My Lai 4 filled with apparent noncombatants.

Commanding officer William Calley reportedly ordered the elderly, women, and children gathered up into groups during search of the village for contraband and Viet Cong forces. Based on an interview with Sergeant Michael Bernhardt "We met no resistance and I only saw three captured weapons. It was just like any other Vietnamese village-old papa-sans [men], women and kids. As a matter of fact, I don't remember seeing one military-age male in the entire place, dead or alive." Despite the facts on the ground and some officers asserting they tried to resist commands from higher-ranking leaders, the orders to eradicate any possible Viet Cong stood.

Calley ordered his men to begin executing the villagers despite a lack of any direct proof of associations with the Viet Cong. According to one report mother's shielding children were shot, children that tried to run were shot, and some among Charlie Company raped women and young girls before killing them. Huts were set ablaze and pillaging soldiers cut down livestock in the massacre as one observing soldier who refrained from combat stated "I saw them shoot an M79 (grenade launcher) into a group of people who were still alive. But it was mostly done with a machine gun."[xciii] No weapon was ever used by a villager against the attacking soldiers and the only reason the bloodshed ended sparing any survivors was the intervention of a United States Army Reconnaissance mission.

Mission pilot Hugh Thompson and his companions spotted the ongoing carnage and landed to separate huddled survivors from approaching soldiers. As the helicopter's machine gunner covered the approaching soldiers, Thompson blocked their advance and threatened to open fire on Charlie Company if they did not cease attacking. Thompson and his crew would transport dozens of survivors from My Lai to receive shelter and medical care.[xciv] Despite Thompson's complaints filed with the Army the My Lai massacre was for a time covered up and he would suffer internal military backlash for proven heroism. Generations subsequent Thompson returned to speak with those he saved in My Lai and one woman among the survivors asked him why those who committed the massacre had not returned with him. Thompson was devastated until she finished her statement by offering that if they returned forgiveness awaited them and this choice to pardon such wanton cruelty overcame him.

The My Lai massacre reportedly killed hundreds of Vietnamese women, children, and elderly people because some were suspected of being Communist or allied with the Viet Cong. Nearly two hundred women, almost twenty of them pregnant, over fifty infants, and several elderly people were murdered in this moment of eternal darkness within the greater shadows of the Vietnam War. Sergeant Bernhardt believes poor treatment embittered his company, extended time in the unforgiving jungles pushed them to their physical limitations, and the recent loss of troops was a compounding mental storm of rising aggression. These factors working in unison incited their fear and disgust mechanisms to seek violence using rationally unjustifiable means guided by the animalistic need for vengeance.

Such massacres are the seeming culmination of several American military policies "to aim for a high body count" engaging our biological expectation for reward and setting the stage for greater violence. To motivate greater body counts in Vietnam "competitions were held between units to see who could kill the most. Rewards for the highest tally, displayed on 'kill boards' included days off or an extra case of beer. Their commanders meanwhile stood to win rapid promotion. Very quickly the phrase- 'If it's dead and Vietnamese, it's VC'- became a defining dictum of the war and civilian corpses were regularly tallied as slain enemies or Viet Cong." Some American leaders and forces had wholly succumbed to collective violence by using lethal force on targets with increasing disregard for civilian deaths. As the unjustified murders accumulated, the Vietnamese public grew increasingly hostile and claims of liberation faded into the reality of violent occupation. Yet My Lai was just the beginning.

Widespread brutality such as My Lai were being replicated as civilians "were killed for running from soldiers or helicopter gunships that fired warning shots, or being in a village suspected of sheltering Viet Cong...The phrase 'kill anything that moves' became an order on the lips of some American commanders whose troops carried out massacres across their area of operations."[xcv] The 9th Infantry Division led by General Julian Ewell began a large operation in the villages of South Vietnam's Mekong Delta. Ewell's troops undertook repeated search and destroy missions with a reported an enemy body count of nearly eleven thousand but captured only seven hundred and fifty weapons. General Ewell's troops according to a United States internal military investigation killed an estimated seven thousand Vietnamese civilians by the end of these operations and this significantly dwarfs the madness at My Lai. Such critical destabilizing mistakes would culminate in millions of Vietnamese deaths and greater than fifty thousand Americans lost in the course of the war. Following the American withdrawal Communist forces took control and reunified Vietnam over twenty years subsequent to the initial hostilities. The next intentional political destabilization occurred via clandestine means a world away from Vietnam in Brazil.

During 1964, the United States Ambassador to Brazil Lincoln Gordon provided detailed political assessments while urging the American government to prevent the alleged rise of a Communist dictator in Brazil. American officials did not support Brazilian President Joao Goulart because of reported associations with the Brazilian Communist Party. When Brazilian society began to unravel, Gordon urged his superiors to provide weapons to local forces serving General Castello Branco to overthrow the current leadership. United States Undersecretary of State Joseph Ball and Assistant Secretary for Latin America Thomas Mann apprised President Lyndon Johnson in a subsequent discussion on supported developments in Brazil and Johnson backs the military coup to remove Goulart in a recorded conversation.[xcvi] Two days later another Central Intelligence Agency cable reported that Goulart was deposed and retreating into exile following the successful military coup.[xcvii]

A CIA summary of the next plot reviewed began "In the 1960s and the early 1970s, as part of the US Government policy to try to influence events in Chile". "The overwhelming objective-firmly rooted in the policy of the period-was to discredit Marxist-leaning political leaders, especially Dr. Salvador Allende, and to strengthen and encourage their civilian and military opponents to prevent them from assuming power." More succinctly, the United States sought to force Chile to assume a government that closer aligned to its national security goals. The American government funded over a decade of paramilitary and propaganda efforts supporting anti-Marxist groups that eventually totaled over six million dollars. Eventually following a botched kidnapping attempt and years of abortive plots, the military plotters successfully overthrew the elected government of President Salvador Allende with backing from the United States government.[xcviii] However, American officials' utilization of grossly disproportionate force was not constrained to merely foreign targets or governments but locally in other instances.

A domestic standoff with a black liberation group is among the most brutal tales of modern America following the political tumult of the 1960s. The Philadelphia and New York based MOVE group embraced communal living, deindustrialization, and anarchistic ideals under the leadership of advocate John Africa. During 1978 after repeated negative interactions between neighborhood locals and MOVE, a deadly confrontation happened amid gunfire. "The first major confrontation between MOVE and the police led to a shootout in Powelton Village...that left Officer James J. Ramp...dead and nine MOVE members in jail for life."

"The incident began when police arrived to execute a court order requiring the group to vacate a compound...after repeated complaints from neighbors concerning the number of animals being kept on the property". Locals further reported "...frequent use of a bullhorn to transmit lectures based on John Africa's teachings, weapons, code violations, the presence of children in reportedly filthy conditions, and MOVE's refusal to pay gas and water bills." The violence injured seven police officers, three MOVE members, five firefighters, and three bystanders.

The deadly events did not deter MOVE from attempting to force the largely black middle-class neighborhood around them to embrace their political agenda. "Move members broadcast their message night and day through a bullhorn from their fortified headquarters. They built what was essentially a fortress within the Osage home, adding bunkers inside the house and on the roof. They also kept many animals-from domesticated dogs and cats to wild rats--in the home, leading neighbors to complain of filth and health risks to both the MOVE children and the neighborhood in general. Observers noted young children who were not enrolled in school. Some neighbors complained of verbal and physical assaults committed by MOVE members and garbage being piled up around the home. As a result District Attorney Edward Rendell issued arrest warrants and Mayor Wilson Goode sent the police to execute the warrants". As expected, MOVE would not respond to the warrants or send the children out from their home. MOVE's disregard for lawful orders, public fear, official disgust for the group, and years of escalating incitement by the factions would bring the situation to a boil in 1985.

It began with police blaring from a loud speaker "Attention MOVE: This is America!", soon fire hoses were flushing the building with a deluge of water and following no response officials broke holes in the structure and fired tear gas. Gunfire ensued between the two sides as thousands of rounds struck the "MOVE compound" and the hail of bullets not only prevented firefighters entering but prevented MOVE members from leaving or surrendering. Police escalated their offensive by using a helicopter to drop C-4 explosives onto the bunker and this caused fires accelerated by stored weapons and gasoline to incinerate the structure. Officials determined saving the house was not worth the risk to firefighters and permitted it to burn thereby inadvertently causing other structures to ignite before live media crews. "The bombing of the MOVE compound killed six adults and five children and destroyed more than sixty homes, leaving more than 250 Philadelphians homeless." A committee appointed by Mayor Goode found authorities had utilized "grossly negligent" tactics when they decided to drop "a bomb on an occupied row house."[xcix] A later Justice Department review agreed that improperly trained police should not have used military equipment against citizens.

No official faced prosecution for the MOVE bombing and the citizens of Philadelphia reelected the mayor, the only person convicted of a related crime was MOVE survivor Ramona Africa. Disputes about the actions of MOVE and officials have led to each side blaming the other for the massacre; however, MOVE is not justified for ignoring legal calls to surrender, years of legal violations, intimidating neighbors, or using violence against officials or locals. Conversely, Philadelphia officials should have contained the area properly, never have used unnecessary lethal force or military grade explosives, and they should have not been reelected because they risked the lives and homes of innocent citizens. Fear and disgust mixed with political beliefs overcame the rational thoughts of those involved and resulted in multiple tragedies because primal motivators establish the road to collective violence and expanding the size of the traumatic event will increase the potential for escalation.

Following the September 11, 2001 attacks targeting the United States by international terrorists, American officials were still reeling from the implications of so many national security failures. As military operations in Afghanistan targeting the Taliban and the network of Osama Bin Laden were ongoing, the political atmosphere of outrage allowed some officials to start another war that had fewer rational justifications. This engagement would eventually cost trillions of dollars, hundreds of thousands of lives, and create a power vacuum that allowed better-organized terrorists to gain power. The Second Persian Gulf War despite the many claims of its proponents was a costly mistake and its effects still devour the resources and lives of Americans in the present. It began with the cessation of diplomacy in 2003 with President George W. Bush issuing a demand that Iraqi dictator Saddam Hussein leave Iraq in forty-eight hours. A possible motivation for this bold threat was due to allegations the Iraqi leader prior dispatched assassins to kill Bush's namesake at a celebration years past in Kuwait. The report of this alleged occurrence had already spurred former President Bill Clinton to order the launch of twenty-three Tomahawk missiles at the headquarters of Iraqi intelligence groups.[c] The battle against the government of Saddam Hussein was rapidly successful and required a timely stabilization effort and eventual withdrawal similar to the first Persian Gulf War undertaken by Bush's predecessor George H.W. Bush.

Unfortunately, the administration of President George W. Bush decided on a long-term occupation of Iraq with an evolving series of justifications for maintaining a dominant military presence despite the unreliable original allegations concerning weapons of mass destruction. Many decisions regarding the occupation would prove disastrous, for instance the American refusals to use most prior officials in the new government or military. With the rise of Shia leaders in the new government, many in the disenfranchised formerly ruling Sunni minority became extremists and launched campaigns of terrorism in response. Another unforeseen consequence of the occupation was

Iraqi Sunni militiamen uniting with other terrorist elements to form new threats. The Persian Gulf occupation continued into the following Obama presidency and a smaller force now endures during the Trump administration.

We further approach a second decade of America seeking to defeat the remaining pockets of terrorist resistance in Iraq but now it faces the Iraqi government's requests to withdraw all forces. It may be this young democratic government in Iraq tires of facing local outrage by the sometimes-heavy-handed operations of United States officials. With most Americans and Iraqis opposing a continued American military presence how many years will it take to escape this endless quagmire? How many decades must be spent in a war that cannot be forever waged and thus cannot be forever won?

The Iraq mistake was just one of multiple almost ceaseless foreign entanglements that include President Barack Obama allowing the CIA to join Islamic fighters and incite the Syrian Civil War. They sought to overthrow Bashar Al Assad but when this failed and the jihadists splintered into groups, among them was the Islamic State (ISIS). This necessitated the redeployment of troops to fight ISIS in the power vacuum left following the second Iraq and Syrian wars. While ISIS terrorists are now largely in retreat, the lives and resources already lost to defeat them would not have been required if the nation building had not occurred. Unites States President Trump's hopeful statements about possibly attempting to withdrawal from Syria and Afghanistan have met bi-partisan rebuke from United States congressional leaders. Unsurprisingly, he did not learn from his predecessors and sent American troops to aid the Saudi government in Yemen seeking to purge its religious enemies similar to their aims in Syria.

Trump himself is no stranger to the desire for immediate retaliation if allegations that he considered assassinating Syrian dictator Assad following a chemical attack on civilians are reliable. According to journalist Bob Woodward the American president told former Defense Secretary James Mattis, "Let's fucking kill him! Let's go in. Let's kill the fucking lot of them".[ci] Mattis reportedly feigned agreement and told the President he would begin assassination planning but told his aide the United States military would not engage in political assassination. It is likely Mattis had read or learned about the past mistakes official groups committed attempting to utilize political assassinations. The Trump administration presumably opted to use air strikes rather than political assassination but the lower brain's early influence clearly expressed itself within the immediate call for clandestine murder.

There is no moral justification for political coups undertaken or aided by the United States government but it seemed to approach domestic and foreign targets at least with some consideration to preventing widespread enduring disorder. The United States and other world powers have toppled multiple foreign governments in measures to protect influence, security interests, and seize desired territory. Similar to the Soviets a number of American officials repeatedly intimidated, threatened, and breached the legal rights of their citizens. Yet one clear line of distinction between the superpowers is that America never legally sanctioned the systematic murder of its own citizens for generations. I am sure this brings little comfort to the many victims of illegal United States government programs worldwide but this important distinction clarifies the path to dominance each nation chose. Our base animal instincts observably seek public dominance and reinforce territoriality; they are what a government values not just based on politics but our biological and social tendencies. Some lines once crossed might change us forever.

CHAPTER 4:

NOTABLE RUSSIAN VIOLENCE

"Those who serve us poison will eventually swallow it themselves." - **Vladimir Putin, former KGB officer and President of the Russian Federation**

The founding revolutionary principals of Communist Russia favored collective rights over the rights of the individual. Despite this goal, a political order similar to the prior oppressive Russian nobility developed with the centralization of power in the Bolshevik leadership and later ruling Communist bureaucrats. A nearly all-powerful Communist dictator would later replace the monarch of old and each system offered a similar extensive misery for the poor. Consequently, declarations of serving the people masked the dictates of subsequent ruling communist leaders and the emergence of monstrous authoritarians would destroy most traces of the revolutionary spirit under the heel of legally mandated tyranny.

The Bolshevik Revolution overthrew the imperial Russian Czar's regime during 1917 with multiple ideological leaders but eventually the most influential was Vladimir Lenin. Bolsheviks did not just destroy the Czarists but also opposition revolutionary leaders who established a weak provisional government with more democratic ideals that did not conform to the Bolshevik dictates. "Lenin's vision of Soviet Russia as a 'fortress besieged by world capital' marked a new phase in the country's centuries-old mistrust of the West, which became synonymous with the bourgeois enemy. His implied dichotomy resonated with a population raised on stories of Polish intrigue, Napoleon's invasion in 1812 and the European powers' aggression during the Crimean War in the 1850s." The Bolsheviks faced incursion by the Allied powers of World War I that sought alliance with their internal opposition. The transforming Bolshevik leadership used a later attack upon the influential Lenin by a young female socialist party member to justify mass murder. Without proving the alleged assassin Fanny Kaplan was responsible for the attack, "she was executed days later-a convenient scapegoat for a regime both under enormous duress and keen to demonstrate its resolve to outsiders. With Lenin incapacitated, and the Bolshevik government shaken by the successful assassination of Petrograd's secret-police chief, Moisei Uritsky, that same day, calls for an extreme response to the 'White Terror' grew louder."

The "Whites" was a term used frequently on any detractor of communist enforced socialism in the early days of the October Revolution. "Under attack on all fronts, including from peasants unhappy with the coercive measures taken to distribute their grain from the countryside to the towns and cities-and with Lenin's life now in the balance, Soviet Russia was about to detonate." The Russian state media publicly demonized any suspected of being a "white" or sympathetic to their dissension. "A frenzied article inciting violence appeared in Pravda exclaiming: "the time has come for us to crush the bourgeoisie or be crushed by it... The anthem of the working class will be a song of hatred and revenge!" The Krasnaia Gazeta newspaper told citizens "only rivers of blood can atone for the blood of Lenin and Uritsky." An environment pervasive with government approved fear and the disgust of traitorous enemies hiding among the populace caused many people to lash out. Days following the attempt on Lenin mobs executed hundreds of people in Petrograd and less than a week passed until the government publicly sanctioned the first mass targeting of White Russians.

The Red Terror

"The Red Terror" was a designed aggression carried out by Lenin and the Bolsheviks to eliminate anyone who stood against their express mandate for socialism and communistic ideals. This decree "prescribed 'mass shooting' to be inflicted without hesitation'..." and the Cheka secret police sprang into action targeting a massive amount of people with torture and execution for their subjectively determined status in a social class. A leading member of the Cheka told his officers "We are not waging war against individual persons. We are exterminating the bourgeoisie as a class...In this lies the significance and essence of the Red Terror."[cii] About fifteen thousand people according to one report perished in roughly a year before Bolshevik leaders extended amnesty to those who remained for a time. These acts foreshadowed the approaching tidal wave of Russian state authored genocide when power fell largely into the hands of a single leader.

One challenge of the young nation was overthrowing the command style imperial economy in Czarist Russia and its forcible transformation into a socialist economy under the Soviet Union. Socialism is the economic idea that workers via the government control all the means of production and set the value of labor. In this system, the will of a small group of influential leaders decides a person's talents, job, and the allocation of profits created. The majority of money a person generates is not theirs but controlled by the government, instead they receive a percentage deemed officially acceptable for all people. Socialism artificially creates

125

values controlled by the governing leaders and philosophies that require the overthrow of existing economies to usher in socialism under the pretense that its benefits outweigh any present economic doctrine. However, this relies on total control of job assignments and forced labor similar to other prior examples of failed economic systems.

While some economic criticisms offered by socialists are valid, instead of repairing or innovating current economics they seek to overturn functional economies for the sake of "progress". This destroys chances for innovation and economic growth because in seizing the production from experts and those versed in the related business you remove all this knowledge from the system and give the system to the less skilled. Socialism then assumes these people can produce on a scale the former experts did without training, experience, and necessary related education. This causes the government to insist on forcing unwilling experts to comply, use non-experts when no experts remained, and in the face of dwindling resources government enforcers resort to violence and oppression. As the system fails, leaders punish innocent workers for the flawed nature of legally enforced policies and blame the people for the foreseeable leadership mistakes. The destruction of a successful economic system causes widespread destabilization and requires more effort than merely correcting a system's flaws. Yet since there is usually no effective way to redress systemic grievances in such countries, a person cannot fix the broken economic ideology that has captured them.

The usual political system favored in socialist economies such as Russia, China, or North Korea is a form of Marxism or Communism; such politics establishes the rich as enemies and relies on promoting class warfare to destabilize nations. Under the assertions of Karl Marx, communists believe they have the duty to attack systems they define as evil or contrary to their ideas. They envision a system of total utopian control without money or classes, yet communists and socialists fail to realize the intrinsic failures and horrors these systems alone or paired have wrought in modern history. Russia is just one example, China's leader Chairman Mao incited the "Great Leap Forward" at the expense of tens of millions of his people lost to famine, and North Korea's Kim family has been starving its own people to death by malnutrition for decades.

Communist leadership assumes all the power and status normally possessed within an entire society and dispenses it to loyal sycophants while brutally censoring opposition sentiments. There is no way to better yourself based upon talent or skill unless you surrender your will to the ruling class and this unjustly limits natural social advancement because most people are not rulers or cronies to the ruling leadership. No additional rewards exist for exceptional work and this replaces personal ambition with a fear of violence or public demonization for any failure to please the leadership. While a minority of people can rise up in the party hierarchy, for the masses there is no rational point to work harder than anyone else does because the rewards are the same for most workers.

Forced labor cannot achieve the same mental, social, and societal benefits that someone who chooses to labor serving his or her own society does. A person that does not care or hates their job will not perform it as well and those refusing to work or that could not work in the Soviet Union were executed as traitors or faced labor camps to perform years of crippling tasks. No private ownership kept most people in a socialist economic underclass and nearly universal poverty inflicted on citizens is claimed to be equality. Such is the story of the later Soviet Union and the ideological violence of the Red Terror foreshadowed a sea of political blood to come.

Stalin's Great Purge

As the ageing Lenin faded, he was supplanted in power by a rising political figure named Joseph Stalin that quickly sought to bring disaffected territories to heel. Stalin needed convenient enemies to begin his modern expansion of public terror as Lenin had targeted the bourgeoisie and used persistent violence under the guise fulfilling popular will to conceal the Russian state's rampant unjust policies. Leading communists had prior decided that rich farmers or dissidents of collectivization posed a threat and the Bolshevik definition for the enemy "kulaks" became anyone Stalin wished. The Soviets even developed a classification system to separate kulaks of differing status and wealth before equally depriving them of their rights. Communist officials deployed state media and young student agitators to garner support for new repressive measures for the supposed benefit of the people.

Soviet national leadership in Bolshevik fashion deemed the kulaks evil, executed them, and survivors under the collectivist system of land management lost their possessions and land for redistribution to empower the state. Later Soviet laws designed to isolate surviving kulaks criminalized aiding those marked as enemies of the people and rendered them a permanent underclass. Destroying entire sections of the wealthy and middle classes forced remaining workers lacking proper education and experience to do their best under impossible circumstances. As the gears of agriculture production and trade drastically slowed without competent guidance, famine killed millions across Soviet held territory. Since they could not replicate former prosperity, the Russian infrastructure unintentionally withered but other damage would occur by express Soviet intention.

Problems between Russia and Ukraine resulted from centuries of Russian imperial rule followed by Lenin backing the seizure of Ukraine for the Soviet Union. Stalin would brook no challenge to his authority and to curb Ukrainian public opposition Russian leaders engineered the Holodomor, a massive controlled starvation of rebellious areas to achieve forced depopulation. Food shipments to the Ukraine were blocked, military forces guarded its borders, staple food prices soared as shortages wore on and people began to go hungry. Some would travel dozens of miles on foot seeking food and trading valuables for meager amounts of nutritious sustenance and when it could not be had they improvised. They ate mixtures of grasses, twigs, and berries called "weed loaf" and soup from the remnants to survive.[ciii] Other people were not so fortunate and one survivor's account describes their unimaginable plight and the "deathly silence...people weren't even conscious. They didn't want to speak or to look at anything...They thought today that person died, and tomorrow it will be me. Everyone just thought of death."

Nonetheless, death was but a wishful thought for the increasingly desperate that observed the growing practice of cannibalism while seeking to maintain their basic humanity. "Survival was a moral as well as physical struggle. A woman doctor wrote to a friend in June 1933 that she had not yet become a cannibal, but was 'not sure that I shall not be one by the time my letter reaches you.' The good people died first. Those who refused to steal or prostitute themselves died. Those who refused to kill their fellow man died. Parents who resisted cannibalism died before their children did."[civ] Stalin essentially was erasing all nurturing or compassionate people who could not bear to inflict suffering on their fellow citizens. Communism was forcing an intrinsic negative change in the culture of an entire generation and justifying this abomination with politics.

The widespread Soviet use of creeping starvation caused a genocide against the Ukrainian people and was just a single example of ruthless policies that led to increasingly violent Russian domination methods. Despite rebel letters describing some of the evolving crimes against humanity to American leaders, Franklin D. Roosevelt and his many Russia enamored advisers began to engage Soviet representatives in further diplomacy the same years the Holodomor occurred. The United Nations extended diplomatic recognition of the growing Union of Soviet Socialist Republics as millions of people starved in the Ukraine or took unthinkable measures to survive. This bleak history is often ignored by some eager to heap praise on flawed ideology that influenced repeated genocides.

Political assassination was a separate tactic Stalin wielded across the Soviet Union to achieve immediate terror and submission. The murder of a popular figure could facilitate a state approved excuse for international war or vast political attacks to purge the established political structure of undesirables. During 1934, a lone political dissident reportedly assassinated Stalin's political rival and Bolshevik leader Sergei Kirov. This event provided the opportunity for Stalin in 1936 to insinuate a grand conspiracy of anti-Stalinist forces allowing him to slaughter his opponents for two years. Among the first political targets were Bolshevik leaders with greater claims to the original revolution in which Stalin was but a minor terrorist figure. Seeking to increase his status and dominate Russia, the Man of Steel began a series of unjust trials followed by the eradication of countless citizens and these sweeping acts of destruction culminated in the Great Purge. The Purge was similar to the Great Terror that gripped France after its revolutionary government turned on its own populace and the Russian purge targeted people with false arrest and mass executions to combat alleged dissidents. Stalin relied on his secret police to undertake this wanton aggression in a concealed manner before any significant public opposition was possible.

The NKVD (People's Commissariat for Internal Affairs) Soviet intelligence group created the Directorate of Special Tasks in 1936 for "terror purposes", among these was conducting assassination. The military group sent out reconnaissance teams into the Russian countryside to assess and begin the execution of Stalin's enemies now labeled fifth columnists and spies. Each round of murders only put Stalin's mind at ease temporarily and to consolidate all power he ordered increasingly barbaric acts of violence using Soviet intelligence groups. The dictator's orders had the opposite effect desired by creating greater dissent and each massacre of his detractors provoked disgust with his methods.

Various high Communist officials to the lowliest members of the public were purged under the cover of politically motivated trials and most Red Army and Navy officers were killed for disloyalty to Stalin's vision following the initial round of murders. Tens of thousands of military personnel died because they did not completely submit to Stalin's changing demands for loyalty or made him suspicious. No Russian citizen was safe from the reach of its Communist tyrant and no crime was required to die but just the perception of impropriety. It required a certain kind of monster to oversee the insatiable need for aggression Russia's Communist dictator exhibited and that particular creature was in a Soviet territory practicing his own brand of violence professionally.

The later head of Stalin's NKVD secret police Lavrentiy Beria was a native Georgian like Stalin, and the former joined the NKVD during 1938. Beria quickly rose to lead to the organization via feeding Stalin's paranoia and was experienced in terror from his background in politically motivated purges of Georgian dissidents while leading its division of the Checka secret police. The Georgian torturer embraced Stalin's bloodlust and served compiling lists of targets for the Russian military police to kidnap or dispatch. Stalin later decreed families be held legally responsible for the crimes of male family members which increased state execution to new levels of immoral depravity and Beria oversaw these massacres absent remorse because he was an expert on human suffering.

Beria according to one report walked the streets of Moscow and when he observed a Russian teenage girl he desired, the NKVD would kidnap and transport her to Beria's estate. They locked the victim in a room until Beria sexually brutalized them and he executed and concealed some of their bodies in the walls of his residence. A few accounts note that Beria allegedly raped dozens of teenage girls and encouraged female relatives of imprisoned or condemned Russians to trade sex for the possibility of leniency. The alleged serial rapist leader of the NKVD determined who lived and died for years and government terror not merit provided him the public status to enact his crimes. Soviet Premier Stalin summarily executed hundreds of thousands by the end of a series of state ordered purges using his criminal minion. Yet at least the dead could no longer suffer the fate awaiting those millions sent for years or decades to the Gulag.

Gulags were dozens of prisons constructed in the tundra of the Russian landscape to contain political dissidents, create a force of free labor (slaves), and render extreme suffering that ended in the death of more than a million Russians. Beria used dissidents to construct and fill the ranks of the growing system of work camps to fuel Russia's faltering economy. One surviving victim of the Gulag labor camps was Red Army officer and later author Aleksandr Solzhenitsyn that composed a disturbing look into his captivity. "First, you defend your homeland against the Nazis, serving as a twice-decorated soldier on the Eastern front in the criminally ill-prepared Soviet Red Army." "Then you're arrested, humiliated, stripped of your military rank, charged under the auspices of the all-purpose Article 58 with the dissemination of 'anti-Soviet propaganda', and dragged off to Moscow's infamous Lubyanka prison." "Then you're sentenced, in abstentia, to eight years of hard labor (but you got away easy; it wasn't so long afterwards that people in your position were awarded a 'tenner'- and then a quarter of a century!)"

Communist officials enraged by the public exposure of the Gulag camps following Solzhenitsyn's release ordered the secret police to poison him but he survived. The author states his book "The Gulag Archipelago" presents "the absolute and utter corruption of the dogmas and doctrines" of Russia, the Soviet Union, its leadership, and himself. Communist leaders exiled Solzhenitsyn from the Soviet Union and they revoked his citizenship but his account exposed supposed collectivist "ethical and philosophical credibility" that created the nightmare he survived. A related description of this Soviet oppression states the Communist empire "ruled in the most corrupt manner imaginable" and was "reliant on the slavery and enforced deceit of its citizens". Solzhenitsyn reportedly "demonstrated that the death of millions and the devastation of many more were...a direct causal consequence of the philosophy (worse, perhaps: the theology) driving the communist system. The "doctrines of Karl Marx contained hidden within them sufficient hatred, resentment, envy and denial of individual culpability and responsibility to produce nothing but poison and death when manifested in the world."[cv cvi]

One important NKVD victim was Leon Trotsky a contemporary and co-founder of the Communist Revolution with Vladimir Lenin; however, he would not relent to Stalin and became a radical enemy of the Soviet government. After one failed attempted to kill Trotsky using a Lithuanian assassin, the NKVD employed deep cover agent Ramon Mercader to charm his way into Trotsky's villa in Mexico City over the course of several months. When Mercader finally gained access and was alone with Trotsky he brutally assassinated him with an ice pick, "...the killing was intended to send a clear message to traitors". For this violent loyalty to communism, Mercader received the title "Hero of the Soviet Union" and the phrase "sending a Mercader" is still a euphemism for employing assassins in Russia.[cvii]

Stalin eventually appointed Lavrentiy Beria Deputy Prime Minister and following the subsequent defeat of Nazi Germany, the secret police chief possessed vast networks of censors and propaganda outlets. Officials constantly revised Russian history, censors destroyed public records, altered photographs, people asking questions vanished, and the Russian state obliterated all of them from memory. Those who dared to ask questions vanished until no one concerned with their own survival made further inquiries. The Stalin regime enjoyed a largely dominated public conditioned with a fear of spies and reeling from terror honed to a fine Soviet edge. Yet we all must eventually face an enemy that cannot be dominated and death by complications from a stroke killed Joseph Stalin. The origins of the stroke are still debated to have been natural causes and others support the possibility that a growing rift between Stalin and Beria might have forced the NKVD chief to poison his superior.[cviii]

Beria's overreaching ambitions led to his death following Stalin's when he sought to repair his public image with a rolling back of Stalin's worst policies; this act inspired the rest of the ruling leaders to execute him for treason against the state. The enduring legacy of Stalin and Beria were the vast purges and violations of the Russian citizenry in name of supposed progress. They and the officials of the Soviet Union systematically wiped out entire generations over the course of endless political murders. These murders would cripple the Russian military because Stalin's orders did not rely on anything more than his politics and this system valued blind loyalty over merit. The Purge's aftereffects further hampered the economic and educational structure of the Soviet Union as well by killing many Russian academics, poets, artists, and philosophers while others tried to flee the Communist regime. Infrastructure and industry weakened as the engineers and technical experts who disagreed with Stalin's repressive measures fell before them. While Stalin did emerge as the dominant force in Russia, it entailed brutally destroying some of the best parts of Russian society.

It was only the rise of a German threat and the Second World War raging Stalin turned some of his brutal impulses from his own people to the Germans. Stalin deployed millions of barely supplied and armed troops to slow the German advance in unison with the ravages of the Russian winter. The Fourth Directorate of the NKGB, a predecessor group to the KGB, undertook World War II terror campaigns targeting Germany by utilizing among the earliest and most proficient sniper corps in modern history that included skilled female sharpshooters. The successes and deficiencies of intelligence and paramilitary groups during the war forced similar restructuring in the Soviet Union that was also occurring within United States intelligence groups.

Following this period, another short-lived intelligence group the MGB replaces the NKGB and it eventually becomes the KGB. The KGB's internal group that dealt with assassinating Soviet enemies was "designated the Thirteenth Department of the KGB Intelligence Directorate (First Chief Directorate)." American intelligence officials report the Thirteenth Department was organized into sections based on countries and groups of nations "...for example, the United States ('the principal enemy'), England, Latin America, etc. At Moscow headquarters the department has approximately 50-60 experienced employees", thus dozens of assassins and terror agents were ready for dispatch worldwide at the KGB's Moscow headquarters. "In addition to headquarters personnel, the 13th Department has its own support officers in legal residencies in Western countries and in some Satellite countries...One of the more active groups is a unit in East Germany which number perhaps 20-30 persons." According to the document before "1955 there was also a group in Austria...As of 1960 there was a group in China, but it probably no longer exists."

Such methods naturally attracted the notice of later American intelligence and one Central Intelligence Agency paper inspecting the Soviet use of assassination states, "It has long been known that the Soviet state security service (currently the KGB) resorts to abduction and murder to combat what are considered to be actual or potential threats to the Soviet regime. These techniques, frequently designated as 'executive action' and known within the KGB as 'liquid affairs'...can be and are employed abroad as well as within the borders of the USSR. They have been used against Soviet citizens, Soviet émigrés and even foreign nationals. A list of those who have fallen victim to such action over the years...would include even the co-founder of the Soviet State Leon Trotsky." As prior noted even the founders of the Soviet nation did not escape the eventual rise of new leadership who considered them ideological threats and thus enemies worthy of death.

"Executive action is also triggered by any signs of possible disloyalty on the part of Soviet officials abroad. The Soviets have gone to great lengths in the past to silence their intelligence officers who have defected, as evidenced by the assassination of former state security officer Ignace Reiss...and the unexplained 'suicide' of former military intelligence officer Walter Krivitsky." Other tactics included the KGB portraying a dissident intelligence official as being insane and taking them into custody for their own protection but this was not limited to the Soviets; their Western counterparts too utilized kidnapping and incarceration to secure intelligence objectives. Yet the Soviet commitment to tracking and destroying all threats and even possible intelligence risks with extreme prejudice diverged from normal clandestine operations.

"The sudden disappearance or unexpected death of a person known to possess anti-Soviet convictions immediately raises the suspicion of Soviet involvement. Because it is often impossible to prove who is responsible for such incidents, Soviet intelligence is frequently blamed and is undoubtedly credited with successes it actually has not achieved. On the other hand, even in cases where the Soviet hand is obvious, investigation often produces only fragmentary information, due to the KGB ability to camouflage its trail. In addition, Soviet intelligence is doubtless involved in incidents that never become officially recognized as executive action, such as assassinations which are recorded as accidents, suicide, or natural deaths."

Thus, any intelligence group utilizing assassination is worthy of at least nominal consideration when a verifiably suspicious death occurs. If Russian officials killed the right person, it could justify nearly any desired unjust policy under defensive or security concerns. Unfortunately, the modern explosion of politically suspicious deaths claims even regarding critics of minor importance often rely on speculations without evidence. The unintentional and planned mixing of highly unlikely deaths with reasonable candidates further conceals these matters by generating false leads. We must balance what the evidence reveals against the benefit and risk of targeting the victim in historical and modern cases

Soviet assassination techniques according to official documents had evolved from the use of firearms and explosives commonly during World War II to more subtle means such as poison and drugs. Former Soviet assassin turned defector Nikolai Khokhlov himself survived a dose of largely traceless radiated thallium administered by Russian intelligence agents. He detailed support laboratories used by the KGB's Thirteenth Department that produced weapons, explosives, drugs, and poisons for "special tasks".[cix] One NKVD lab Khokhlov referred to conducted experiments on prisoners for testing various poisons and chemical agents. The NKVD conducted tests using arsenic, cyanide, thallium, atropine, barbiturates, and chloral hydrate and later employed select mixtures to kill and immobilize victims targeted by Russian intelligence services. The NKVD's medical section, the Kamera, had years prior developed "lethal toxins" that included a gel initiating a heart attack when exposed to the victim's skin.

The CIA learned of another "unique mechanism for administering poison" using "a pneumatically operated poison ice 'atomizer' which leaves no wound or other evidence of the cause of death." This would allow the plotting agents to assassinate someone and leave far less evidence or indication that a nefarious act had occurred. Khokhlov also revealed collaboration between Soviet staff officers mixed with indigenous agents in combat groups that in special circumstances hunted down Soviet political enemies. This wide array of hidden techniques used by guerilla teams or lone assassins demonstrates a large and effective network at the behest of the KGB long before the agencies of rival nations had effectively developed them.

"It is probable such trams are a modern variation of the 'mobile groups' described by a pre-war source as units dispatched from Moscow to foreign countries to assassinate Trotskyites and state security officers who refused to return to the USSR". Many dissident former citizens and imperial Russian expatriates lived abroad constantly protesting the Communist government and Soviet leaders targeted political dissidents for abduction, imprisonment, and murder. "Such operations are sometimes designed to demonstrate that the Soviet regime can strike its enemies anywhere in the world." Using these methods intelligence groups and related governments are empowered to create "fear, unrest, confusion, and dissension" within targeted émigré groups and larger organizations. CIA officials further noted the cases of political assassination that remained hidden for years until Soviet defectors revealed them.

"On the other hand, assassination of some émigré leaders have been carried out so skillfully as to leave the impression that the victims died from natural causes." This is unsurprising because the Soviet governmental apparatus funded and organized such violence using illegal means and was innovating untraceable assassination before the Central Intelligence Agency existed. The massive legal system of rights Western nations established to prevent and counteract such operations did not bind the Soviet Union and while this did not prevent all Western leaders from using assassination seeking to remove foreign threats, it drastically reduced the development of such plots with institutional support. This was in addition to exposure and the consequences outweighing most potential benefits of using overt domination to inspire political changes.

The GRU (Chief Directorate of the Red Army's General Staff) military intelligence group was an independent association that not only sought to destroy the Russian military's enemies but also maintained fierce competition with other allied groups such as the KGB. Central Intelligence Agency case officer Russell Langelle handled intelligence gathered by Pytor Popov a CIA source in the GRU during the late 1950s and Langelle deemed meeting Popov the single most important priority during his service in the Soviet capital. By 1958 official documents state the KGB reassigned Popov to less important work in Berlin under constant surveillance and this prevented him from engaging important sources of intelligence. The GRU discovered its officer Pytor Popov was serving the CIA internally for years when Russell Langelle is apprehended with documents sent by the double agent and the Russian government executes Popov in 1960.[cx]

Russian assassin and defector Bogdan Stashinskiy turned himself in to the West German police and confessed that under Soviet orders he "assassinated two individuals" in the past. He revealed in 1961 the murder of Ukrainian dissident writer Lev Rebet and Ukrainian Nationalist movement leader Stepan Bandera.[cxi] [cxii] Both men were political dissidents who sought to incite Ukrainian separation from the Soviet Union and Russian officials unleashed Stashinskiy to dispatch them. This was a common predicator for Soviet assassination; a critic of Russian policy became nothing less than a target for elimination. However, a public murder can draw unwanted attention or witnesses and later Soviet assassins had much more sophisticated weapons than bombs.

Previously during 1957 Stashinskiy lurked inside the stairway of a building where his target Lev Rebet's office was located seeking to descend past the dissident writer. Stashinskiy walked by Rebet on the stairs holding a specialized weapon concealed within his newspaper until the assassin drew close and produced a slim metallic tube. The weapon fired a mist of poison from a pressurized chamber through a screen that struck Rebet in the face as he inhaled. The assassin continued down the stairs as the victim collapsed and this lethal mist almost instantly paralyzed Rebet's arteries causing his brain or heart to shut down. The victim was quickly dead seemingly from random natural causes while the toxic agent dissipated leaving no trace five minutes later.

Bogdan Stashinskiy later assassinated his victim Stepan Bandera using a double-barreled modified version of the same weapon he used on Lev Rebet. The scenario was almost identical to his last murder; he awaited Bandera inside his apartment building as the Ukrainian political leader arrived home from the grocery store. Stashinskiy positioned himself in the hallway by an elevator near the victim's apartment door. Bandera laden with groceries was struggling to remove his key from the door and

Stashinskiy approached then grasped the door handle seeming to aid Bandera then inquired if the lock was broken. As Bandera confirmed the door worked a lethal mist fired out of the tubes concealed by the assassin's clutched newspaper. Bandera collapsed as his assassin successfully escaped without detection a second time.[cxiii]

Despite the success of those like Stashinskiy employing poison for assassination, poison is a temperamental medium in such fluid situations without extensive training. The slightest miscalculation can render a planned kidnapping into a murder or a failed assassination to mere poisoning and one such example includes the poisoning of Lisa Stein a radio interviewer for Western Germany propaganda outlet Radio in American Sector. Communist intelligence agents used candy infused with the potentially lethal poison scopolamine on Stein because these would-be abductors intended for her to fall unconscious. Ultimately, the poison did not render her unconscious quickly enough and observant neighbors intercepted Stein and sent her to the hospital.

Attempts to poison Radio Free Europe staff by lacing cafeteria saltshakers with atropine which causes death or paralysis was another method attributed to Soviet intelligence.[cxiv] The New York Times report of the attack in 1959 implies those responsible were attempting to maximize victims by using the communal dining area. "The amount of poison in each salt shaker was said to be 2.36% by weight of the contents. White crystalline alkaloid is indistinguishable from salt." This action would further broaden the normally targeted programs of assassination to mass poisoning and murder akin to terrorism. During the 1970s, the prior mentioned heart attack inducing gel targeted anti-Soviet writer Alexander Solzhenitsyn but the lethal toxin failed to kill him. In nineteen seventy-eight, the KGB also targeted Bulgarian playwright dissident Georgi Markov in London with a ricin treated pellet fired by the tip of an umbrella. Reportedly, KGB Chairman Yuri Andropov sanctioned the attack, assigned it to allied Bulgarian forces, and Markov died horribly days following the incident.

One of the most enduring differences concerning Russian and other intelligence group methods of assassination were the standards for doing so. While many groups seemingly would spare no expense in targeting chosen threats, the Russians had different security priorities concerning each target. While the CIA or SIS as a matter of course targeted high value enemy officials with several failed murderous plots based on unnecessary risks, they usually reserved assassination for a more limited number of people weighed against the public blowback. However, in a minute amount of cases, the Soviets did not purge every defector when they recognized a more beneficial propaganda opportunity.

The matter of KGB defector Vitaly Yurchenko is one that demonstrated the Central Intelligence Agency's failure to secure a new valuable defector and provide him the means to better assimilate to Western culture. Yurchenko would provide the Agency with useful intelligence but he later decided to redefect to the Soviet Union and referred to his willing defection as kidnapping by Western intelligence. Not only did this miscast the circumstance of his defection publicly but also likely deterred other intelligence defectors and it is possible the entire defection was merely a false one designed to damage the United States recruitment of future defectors. Yurchenko was one of the few returning to the Soviet Union that lived to ever speak publicly about his experience. One related KGB official commented the defector's survival indicated, "Either Yurchenko is as smart as the devil himself...or he is the luckiest bastard alive." [cxv] In time, all the Soviet government's repressive methods and murderous rage would compound to destabilize the Russian political empire.

The Soviet Union withered as the end of the twentieth century drew near and empty banks, foreign opposition, changing public attitudes, and the newfound will of people yearning for greater individual freedom brought its fall. Public backlash grew toward the leading Soviet authors of past violent oppression and economic crisis gripped the Communist Bloc as the crawl toward democracy began. This seeming advancement beyond some past brutality was a delicate bloom from the infant democratic forces emerging during the dissolution of the Soviet Union. Yet a chilling wind of change swept over and destroyed any significant chance of widespread democracy or economic mobility for most Russians. While the institutions of communism have seemingly fallen and its leaders were scattered, some prior officials had grafted themselves to the new leadership of Russia.

One ambitious former KGB officer named Vladimir Putin emerged quietly following the chaotic transition from Soviet Empire to Russian Federation. Communist Russia fell and was in many ways reconstituted with aid from prior Western enemies as the current Russian Federation. Putin would quickly rise under the Yeltsin government and now Russia sports a fresh strongman at the helm who disregards international law. Putin is a military and intelligence trained cold warrior akin to American leaders of the past with a pronounced contempt for laws that challenge his political agenda. While the Cold War might have ended for most, there is a warm place in the heart of Russia's leading politician for hunting defectors and assassinating enemies of the state. Russia began a new series of aggressions to remain on the cutting edge of public assassination by employing it regularly. The list of Putin critics killed under officially suspicious and politically motivated circumstances is extensive and growing; the targets vary from minor domestic critics to groups of foreign officials.

Russian Parliament member Vladimir Golovlyov received funding from political enemies of Putin and he was a leading member of the opposition Russian Liberal Party. The fifty-four-year-old lawmaker took a morning walk down the street with his dog in 2002 and failed to return home and his body was recovered shortly afterwards with two bullet holes in a nearby Moscow park. Golovlyov's mother told the media political assassinations "give the country a very bad name, proving that lawlessness and criminal outrage are not just empty words in Russia...Regrettably, they have become the reality in our daily life." Golovlyov was the first of dozens of high-profile critics of Putin that were publicly assassinated.

Sergei Yushenkov the Putin critic and founder of the Liberal Russia party had a positive reputation for lending his assistance to prevent a former KGB coup against Soviet leader Mikhail Gorbachev. Hours following a public announcement that his party would take part in upcoming elections an unknown killer shot him near his apartment and one media report presented the differences between Yushenkov and some other political targets by noting his lack of corrupt business practices. Notably he supported allegations that Russia's FSB organization was responsible for apartment bombings in a 1999 terror attack. This act targeted the apartments of Russian military troops and their families later providing a pretext for war against Chechnya. Even Vladimir Putin who many allege is responsible for ordering Yushenkov's assassination stated the deceased man took up the duty of defending "democratic freedoms and ideals." [cxvi] Yushenkov's death marked the tenth politician killed in Russia since 1994 and he was the second member of his minority party targeted.

Repeated media critic Anna Politkovskaya accused the Putin government of corruption, human rights violations, murdering political dissidents in Chechnya, and rendering modern Russia into a police state. An unknown "person" dispatched five contract killers to shoot the reporter in the lobby outside her residence similar to the Yushenkov murder. The Russian legal system determined she was assassinated by members of a conspiracy paid over one-hundred thousand dollars and these men faced incarceration for the reporter's death but multiple people blamed for the conspiracy obtained acquittal. Most telling was the indictment of former Moscow police Lieutenant Colonel Dmitry Pavlyuchenko for orchestrating and being an accomplice to Politkovskaya's murder. Since 2006, assassinations have killed almost two dozen Russian journalists and sixty-three violent attacks have targeted members of the media in Russia.[cxvii][cxviii]

Former KGB and FSB (Russian Federal Security Service) officer Alexander Litvenenko defected the year of Politkovskaya's death to England because of the political reaction to his unmasking of a domestic assassination plot. The English SIS paid Litvenenko to aid investigations targeting the Russian mafia and inquiring about the death of other Putin critics. In November of 2006, Litvenenko had tea with two Russian FSB agents and soon after fell grievously ill; he would suffer and die gruesomely in the hospital following the meeting from the effects of a radioactive substance poured into his drink. This would further affirm a renewed commitment by some Russian leaders to uphold the Cold War hunt for Russia traitors and enemies by any means necessary.[cxix] A 2016 British inquiry regarding the defector's murder implicated Vladimir Putin in his death.

Sergei Magnitsky was a Russian lawyer who blew the whistle on a two hundred and thirty-million-dollar tax fraud being perpetrated by Russian officials and was jailed in 2008 on charges of financial corruption. Russian jailers beat Magnitsky repeatedly during his incarceration for over a year and despite suffering from serious health conditions, they deprived him of medical care. He died after extensive mistreatment in official custody and those responsible "received awards and promotions" while connected leaders undertook a single trial for all the related alleged wrongdoing targeting Magnitsky following his death. It reportedly is the sole Russian legal trial against a dead man on the record and no one faced responsibility but the murdered lawyer that attempted to expose wrongdoing. Magnitsky's suffering inspired his former employer Bill Browder to advocate for a legal package of sanctions for international use against those complicit in human rights abuses. Several Western nations have embraced and now utilize the sanctions to the detriment of those violating human rights.[cxx]

The year Magnitsky was incarcerated the Russian government supported Abkhazi and South Ossetia, two Georgian breakaway provinces, in their legally unrecognized attempt to fall under Russian control. Based on the highly questionable claim that Georgia harbored Chechen militants Russia used allegations to employ military force. This military intervention allowed Russia to gain influence over the two breakaway regions Abkhazi and South Ossetia by recognizing their independence from Georgia.[cxxi] Similar violent encounters between Ukrainian forces and rebels supported by Russian troops left five hundred dead and nearly two thousand people wounded. Both Georgia and Ukraine during that year were under consideration for membership in the European Union but no vote of acceptance or denial occurred. The Putin regime sensing these former Soviet holdings might fall under European influence likely molded the Russian strategy of intervention.

Stanislav Markelov was a Russian human rights attorney that represented a variety of journalists and critics that opposed the Russian control of Chechnya and Vladimir Putin. Among his clients was Novaya Gazeta, the newspaper of Putin critic and assassination victim Anna Politkovskaya and he advised the newspaper on her murder case. Markelov also represented the family of a young kidnapped, raped, and murdered Chechen woman seeking justice against Russian military officer Yuri Budanov. A Russian court revealed Budanov secretly instructed military subordinates to bury the girl and despite this rational attempt to conceal his crime, he claimed temporary insanity. Markelov publicly stated he intended to appeal Budanov's release and would hold a press conference regarding such matters hours before he died.

Following the press conference Markelov and journalist Anastasia Barnurova walked down a street filled with people toward public transportation in the center of Moscow. A lone man in military fatigues emerged from the passing crowd and shot Markelov in the head with a pistol, despite the shocking daylight murder Barnurova chased the assassin. The killer turned and shot the young female giving pursuit in the head without a word despite that shooting Barnurova was not seemingly part of his original plan. Her brave insistence to seek justice for her murdered associate and not allow this killer to vanish as so many others had proved deadly. The family of the murdered girl who the assassinated lawyer represented informed the press shortly before Markelov died that he was receiving threats and phone messages instructing him to stop talking about the Budanov matter. A spokesperson for Human Rights Watch commented on Markelov's death stating, "He is the latest in a long line of strong critics of the state who have got killed."[cxxii]

Human rights advocate and journalist Natalia Estermirova had worked occasionally with reporter Anna Politkovskaya prior to her death on stories critical of growing unrest in Chechnya and Russia. One story Estermirova reported on shortly before her own death alleged that Russian aligned Chechen security forces burned down the houses of suspected rebels. Prior to her assassination, she was collaborating with Human Rights Watch on alleged sensitive cases of human rights violations including the death of a suspect without trial. Four men kidnapped the reporter as she yelled for help near her dwelling and subsequently, they left her corpse in a wooded area fifty miles away. A researcher colleague in

Moscow stated that Estermirova's murder related to her professional activities and the crime remains unsolved.[cxxiii][cxxiv]

A major Russian seizure of land and profitable waterways occurred in 2014 with the annexation of Crimea a former Soviet holding. The history of Crimea's importance stretches back to the nineteenth century when Western imperial nations defeated the Russian empire and forced the dismantling of Russia's major Black Sea port. This cut off Russia from the Black Sea and the Mediterranean and rendered it ineffectual as a naval military power until the Soviet Union reclaimed this area. As the Communist bloc crumbled, the Crimea became a part of the independent country of Ukraine that has attempted to distance itself from Russian influence.

Following such history as the Holomodor, the Ukrainian people are so averse to continued Russian domination they have set up a separate branch of the Orthodox Church with the consent of main church's leadership. Russia in response to the Ukraine's growing political independence has conducted a rolling annexation, following the seizure of the Crimea and its Black Sea port. The Russian regime now in violation of international treaties polices the Sea of Azov despite former agreements with the Ukraine and can block and harass ships traveling to Ukrainian ports. Russian ships have militarily engaged Ukrainian ships and have its small navy outgunned as the reported land and sea annexation push continues.[cxxv] With each new land acquisition, Russia's territory begins to resemble its former Soviet appearance and increasingly tout a desire to strike out at further enemies.

Boris Nemtsov was an outspoken critic of Vladimir Putin and former Deputy Prime Minster of Russia under the government of Boris Yeltsin who repeatedly alleged Putin was in the pocket of the ruling oligarchs. Subsequently as he walked home with his girlfriend from a restaurant near the Kremlin, the bullets of an unknown assailant struck him down. President Putin took "personal control" of the hunt for Nemtsov's murderer and Russian officials deemed five prior Chechen security members guilty of conspiring to kill Nemtsov. Officials deny the murder was politically motivated and ignored significant questions from the dead man's family and members of the public disputing the irregular official investigation that failed to verify a motive. The death of a Putin critic often leads the state to convict those it was already targeting without answering why other convenient enemies would kill a political opponent of the Russian leadership.[cxxvi]

Mikhail Lesin the previous Russian Press Minister that founded the state funded Russia Today network pondered a deal with the United States Federal Bureau of Investigation to avoid legal charges in 2015. Days before he was scheduled to meet with the United States Justice Department, Lesin's was subsequently discovered in a Washington DC hotel room having suffered a lethal head wound. Originally, his death reportedly was due to multiple drunken falls but FBI investigators alleged it resulted from a severe beating gone too far by unknown thugs working on the command of another Russian oligarch. It is quite improbable anyone would dare to beat or murder such a highly placed figure without the consent or acknowledgement of the Kremlin, the Russian seat of political power. The repeatedly brazen public murder of well-known Russia citizens that might endanger Putin's regime is not an aberration but a common practice that continues unabated.

Putin critic and prior Russian legislator that renounced his citizenship Denis Voronenkov fled to the Ukraine with his wife to escape the clutches of the Russian leadership. Criminal allegations following the end of his legislative term would align with several other cases of fabricated charges targeting enemies of the Putin government. Thus, it should be unsurprising that a later assassin shot Voronenkov to death in a daylight attack within the Ukrainian city of Kiev during 2017. A media source commented, "This is almost certainly a political murder ordered by the Kremlin in the longstanding KGB tradition of executing traitors--and a chilling statement of intent from Russian President Vladimir Putin to the Ukrainian government."[cxxvii] . This act further matches the longstanding dogma of the Soviet and Russian states to hunt down and destroy their enemies and betrayers.

During the spring of 2018 Russian KGB defector Sergei Skripal was at the mall in England with his daughter and both of them collapsed. It was later determined the pair were poisoned by Novichok; a nerve agent developed by the Soviet Union to counter American military defenses. Skripal unlike many other defectors was still actively offering information to multiple Western intelligence groups and this likely made him a target. Yet the attack on this defector and his daughter was just the beginning of the matter and it would expand to a worldwide drama in the press. Since Novichok was highly toxic and transmissible, the nerve agent caused multiple health scares when exposing others in areas of prior deployment. So transmissible was the nerve agent that one investigating officer and his family had to abandon every material possession and their home to escape further contamination. The British government has charged two alleged Russian GRU military intelligence agents for the attack that fled to Russia "in abstentia" for "conspiracy to murder, attempted murder, and use of the nerve agent Novichok".[cxxviii]

While modern Russia has thus far killed significantly less people overall than the Soviets, the former leadership at least usually assassinated individuals without potentially targeting a huge mass of innocent foreign civilians if only to escape international detection; the current Russian leadership appears unconcerned with such things. The past intimidation and propaganda value of precise defector assassination loses its effectiveness by a willingness to kill others with no connection to the matter.[cxxix] The Russian leadership might wish to consider the long-term effects of using chemical weapons because Western nations will consider Russia a terroristic threat if they continue to employ chemical warfare that could indiscriminately threaten large populations. Repeated actions by the Putin government do not portend any change in their standard policy of lethally dealing with those considered threats.

A disturbing poll among the Russian people taken during 2018 suggests a majority now regret the fall of the Soviet Union, well at least those who survived it. These sentiments were predicted in the nineteen nineties by American diplomat George Kennan who told the public that increasing NATO's membership would be a "fateful error" that would "inflame the nationalistic, anti-Western and militaristic tendencies in Russian opinion". Kennan warned this political strategy would "restore the atmosphere of the cold war to East-West relations". Under the current leadership that ennobles historic Soviet power many Russians have a desire to regain greater international eminence.[cxxx] [cxxxi]

This yearning for a return to nearly lone superpower status is wholly in keeping with the human pattern and doing so by any means necessary comports to prior Soviet leaders. During two thousand nineteen Russia's parliament approved a bill that legalizes the arrest of people who "disrespect" the Russian government. The "new" law is a revitalization of Soviet era repressions that penalized those committing "anti-Soviet agitation", it weakens the decriminalization of expression under Boris Yeltsin, and returns a Soviet pallor to the allegedly open Russian society. A series of international military conflicts have seemingly reset the clock for decades of fresh icy diplomacy that bear a strong resemblance to dangerous past mistakes.

The government takeover of major media companies in Russia filled the Russian Federation's airwaves with Putin regime approved propaganda and unlike the former Soviet government, the oligarchs did not seize the entire media but instead they acquired it. The very act of belonging to pro-democracy organizations who oppose regime policies can garner criminal charges and lead to extensive imprisonment, if they survive public attempts by unknown assassins to murder them.[cxxxii] The incarceration and torture of several religious dissidents by the Putin government renews a past Communist hatred of some religions in modern Russia.[cxxxiii] The frigid winds of kleptocracy have swept through Russia with nearly all power and influence amassed in the hands of a select group just as the prior Soviet government had been.

The series of Kremlin moves to render modern Russia into a mixture of regressive Soviet style laws and corrupt markets is proving untenable as the years pass. With Putin's attacks on Crimea and Georgia, it might be he seeks to gradually annex every strategic former holding of the Soviet Union in his evolving version of the Russian Federation. This desire for a return to past diplomacy echoes in his latest threat to the United States over conflicts regarding the placement of ballistic missiles. "Russian President Vladimir Putin said Russia is militarily ready for a Cuban Missile-style crisis if the United States wanted one and threatened to place hypersonic nuclear missiles on ships or submarines near the U.S. territorial waters." The extensive sanctions placed on the Russian government have drastically affected the Russian economy and the Putin regime's ability to profit from it; this may be among the factors influencing the Russian president's latest threats.[cxxxiv] Putin's growling has the familiar sound of former Cold War Soviet leader Nikita Khrushchev as he promised to bury his enemies but instead his enemies laid the Soviet government to rest and financially helped save modern Russia.

Echoes of the Great Purge helped form later policy and murder in Russia became a tool of the government. The state mandated killing spree of Russian terror and less frequent purges molded enduring Russian intelligence policies and institutionalized political assassination. Some KGB and Russian officials had no compunctions and evidence suggests a policy of actively targeting anyone deemed a traitor or enemy of value. This use of assassination on such a wide scale had the desired effect of fear but also created a disgruntled class of people unable to voice their political opposition and will likely further inspire more dissension. The latest moves of Russia's government to restrict online speech and access smacks of the past Soviet policing of acceptable public information.[cxxxv]

Repressive Soviet methods proved wasteful and largely ineffective to prevent further betrayal while their propensity for assassination eventually filtered into Western intelligence groups. Opposing leaders believed the only way to fight the Red Menace was to use their worst tools against them in escalating hostilities. Political critics in the Russian Federation may face death or imprisonment because of thought crime if they dare to flee or speak out and this again leaves most of them in a bleak winter of suffering from which not even relocation around the world can protect them. All these inhuman practices grew from the nature of humans and the environment such humans existed within. The Russian Federation and the United States appear locked within the intrigues begun during the last century seeking to fulfill policy created by cold warriors long dead. Their desire for competitive dominance without regard to future consequences leads to unquestionable suffering internationally.

CHAPTER 5:

DEFYING AGGRESSION AND VIOLENCE

"Violence does, in truth, recoil upon the violent, and the schemer falls into the pit which he digs for another.

" - **Arthur Conan Doyle, Author**

Despite the similar circumstances leading to both the American and Soviet peoples throwing off imperial control, the revolutionary movements in Russia and the United States led to broadly diverging societies. While the founders of the United States largely remain figures of enduring longevity and national pride, most of the original Bolshevik founders faced assassination or exile to consolidate Soviet power in subsequent purges. While the United States has extensive connections to its creators still taught in American schools, the Russians wiped many founding revolutionaries from history at the command of Soviet leaders because they represented ideological challenges. Erasing or suppressing already known history entails drastic eventual consequences when the truth emerges and this authoritarian streak can rise in every type of political system because humans overseeing them seek to dominate competing ideas.

The repeated systematic use of violence by each of these current members of the United Nations Security Council and their failure to protect necessary freedoms in their own nations is a poor example for others to follow. If the strongest nations of the world cannot provide necessary freedom to their citizens, how truly powerful are they? Power does not equate to greatness, wealth and resources can measure economic success but not the quality of a nation. Providing ample individual rights and the ability to determine our personal fate constrained only by reasonable fair laws is the essence of a valuable existence. Only a truly great nation defends the primacy of the individual against the tyrannies of unlawful government.

The difference between democratic republican political systems with capitalist economies and communist political systems with socialist economies measures in the hundreds of millions of lives sacrificed under authoritarian systems. Millions starved in the Ukrainian Holomodor, Gulags, and Chinese reeducation camps remind us of the measurable historical differences. The vast chasm between these political and economic systems features the past genocidal programs of one system and the rapid expansion of the other. Even modern China, the only communist superpower has adopted capitalist economic policies for their beneficial financial and social returns.

Those superpowers prior inspected verify that humans will repeatedly succumb to the oldest and most historically established way to achieve dominance, the use of violence. Presently the dominant powers of the twentieth century face new superpowers on the world stage and geopolitics grows increasingly complex. The rise of Communist China and the European Union have counterbalanced the prior dominant positions held by only two superpowers in the last century and several other smaller nations and groups now attempt to assert regional dominance. Status and fighting to achieve favorable diplomatic and military positions employ increasingly aggressive and violent operations. Citizens often feel similarly to the stance of their nation and our tribal prejudices usually override further inspection of foreign people and groups. Enabled by our fear and disgust mechanisms individuals and political groups can incite greater violence as divisive politics gain traction. Increasing hands rise up to strike out toward perceived inhuman enemies, but a moment of pause is in order.

Before lashing out and submitting to baser instincts or societal pressures, do aggressors consider the basic humanity of those eagerly targeted and what the consequences are when things get out of hand? People currently are disposed to escalation for even a minor perceived disagreement because widely varying beliefs exist about what constitutes offensive behavior. To overcome these pervasive animalistic desires and harness our lower self in the service of greater progress we must break the cycle of aggression and discern the futile nature of needless violence. If we are each too busy fighting and destroying our enemies to have fulfilling lives exactly what is the endgame to all this? If people expect others to behave in a civilized manner, they must first do so.

Civilized people allow dissent and should err on the side of free speech because suppressing criticism based on facts is not rational. Humans require the ability to openly socialize and learn about new information they consider important, when people attempt to restrict speech or knowledge it psychologically inspires a greater desire in others to seek the restricted content. Secret information would not be so inviting if people did not make it secret and gain status by learning such information. The same rationale applies when people attempt to censor legal free speech; if it is perceived as unjust additional disgusted people will oppose and bring attention to related censorship.

If some deem words offensive humans will find ways around censorship and create replacement words, the only way to ban offensive words is to ban all speech and thus all thought. To restrict speech based on offense or government fiat is nothing less than embracing the censorship that was pervasive in Russia during Stalin's tyranny and America during the Red Scare. Our minds naturally shriek out at perceived unfair treatment and in the case of genuine obvious mistreatment, they rail even louder. This widespread fight between censorship and free thought occurs now also beyond the bounds of reality ceaselessly in digital space.

The internet is a manifestation of all the beauty and horror within the human mind representing a ceaseless growing spectacle that has captured most of humanity's imagination. However, it is merely an implement fashioned in the image of normally unseen aspirations or desires that we can choose to set down. One sets it down to engage in other necessary activities because no single implement can be the answer to the range of problems humanity faces. Overreliance upon any one thing violates basic tenets of moderation prescribed by ancient wisdom to be a recommendation in all things. Obsession is self-destructive if left forever unchecked and our seeming modern addiction to social media and entertainment is having serious detrimental effects upon human minds. Any habit-forming activity, similar to drugs, causes pleasure responses in the brain and the longer such activity occurs the deeper the response. Rising mental illness influenced by antisocial digital behaviors, suggest a problem that we cannot afford to let worsen by inaction.

A digital environment is in part a false one, social media or online conflicts can only influence and affect reality if humans allow them to translate to real life. Status and attention earned online is largely meaningless in the real world to many people, it cannot save you from attackers, it cannot feed or clothe you, and it cannot provide the required direct interaction with others that promotes human mental health. Legions of online followers can be purchased or simulated and pale to real life supporters that actually promote celebrities to other live people. Unlike earned social status for merit or achievement, people gain and confer online status by an endless amount of varying reasons but many equate to little more than endorsements and fads. Significant amounts of people online are anonymous and do not often participate actively but observe the conflicts started by others because they enjoy the spectacle of fighting and do not care nearly as much about the fighters. No one's real life seems affected in this virtual environment and we do not see the subsequent long-term human consequences. It is as if some have wholly divorced themselves from reality and rational behavior to sink deeper into fantasy leaving us to ponder solutions to these increasingly troubling patterns.

While a person's first inclination based on some evidence might be to abstain from social media completely, it may be easier to reduce time gradually before doing so. It seems reasonable to engage in greater self-regulation of our usage to include only necessary communication activity until the negative aspects of such technology become clearer. Given the detrimental effects feasibly caused by overuse, taking no action is not an option if humanity wishes to mitigate the increasing problems complacency has caused. If we do not address these modern disruptions to our normal mental health, they will get worse and some have begun to embrace their darker biological nature.

We cannot properly regulate our behavior if we consciously fail to limit our deeper instincts from exerting total control. This is not to suggest we should abandon millions of years of defensive evolution to our detriment in some cases but seek to focus it usefully. All humans can perceive someone who is unfamiliar or visually different as threats triggering the lower brain defenses but we must counter that by stabilizing our tendencies with reason in the higher brain. Perhaps it will be possible in the distant future to utilize these diametric opposite areas to work in greater harmony but no single solution can document the road to moderating our primal urges because a greater regimen of learning about our biological selves is still required.

The higher brain tells us to survive we must learn to coexist and place intrinsic value on real human socialization that no technology can replace. Our minds rely on genuine experiences that can offer a range of useful pressures and stressful negative situations that test us on many levels. Our deeper minds have powerful defensive mechanisms with flaws that need the higher brain to regulate them. This requires us to resist our human tendency for conflict, we shall fail at times, but no hope for improvement exists if we are unwilling to give a supreme effort. The stakes cannot be higher if we do not learn to control our destructive tendencies because continuing upon this path of escalating aggression eventually could assure humanity's extinction.

A vital component upon a road to understanding ourselves is considering the billions of other individuals that live on this planet. The largest biological group far exceeds whole nations, governments, genders, religions, political parties, and community organizations. Its membership excludes not a single person on the face of the Earth, it has no rules to join, and no one can revoke your status despite whom you might offend. This most inclusive group is humanity, all people of all lands are members, and the stark divisions present in varying societies usually blot out the common union of the human species. Yet distance, culture, and language do not preclude a single individual worldwide from being a part of this biologically linked family.

Essentially humans are the exact same carbon-based creature with endless minor differences but some allow these differences to define them and others use them as wedge issues to dehumanize rivals. The hatred, aggression, violence, and oppression present around the world does not change that our shared mortality requires that we each be born, strive and fail, rejoice and suffer, and die. Since people are nearly the exact same creature and general combination of biology, we all desire and deserve basic respect. If we desire a better life, do we provide others the same treatment we expect? This is not a reference to some maudlin ideal of being nice to everyone but a suggestion that offering basic respect to others further ensures our survival as a species. Confrontations are less prone to occur; people are more likely to be cooperative with good neighbors because treating people well incentivizes reciprocation. Several noble and selfish reasons exist to do the right thing and to ignore the benefits of cooperation for temporary negative emotional satisfaction is a mistake.

The recognition of common humanity and its direct link with the survival of our species paired with basic civility and the attempt to control our instinctual tendencies would offer stark improvements upon current socialization, especially within the realm of social media. The road each formerly discussed superpower took are but two of the many every nation might tread but the notable similarities and differences are telling and offer greater insights why some ideas merely persist and others change the world. If we actively form new patterns, it can translate into new habits and behaviors and this can over great periods change our societies by engaging the reason of people and not seeking to incite the lower brain to attack people perceived as threats. Ultimately, it should be the decision of every free person to choose their own speech and those attempting to force conformity of thought upon those who disagree will only cause greater public disaffection. Force and threats cannot erase the natural desire of all animals to be free, we are humans but we are animals as well.

Humanity must severely reduce violence to endure beyond the next millennia within a legally balanced social framework. However, we must determine the best methodology and path to assure this while maintaining free societies that respect individual rights and do not censure unpopular thought. Uncomfortable topics of debate cause some people stress, but stress is more than a consequence of our existence. It is a mechanism to ensure our survival and being perpetually comfortable is not a natural state of existence and denies our primal desire to strive and excel. The pressure of possible failure is a natural consequence of exerting our minds and bodies; the person without it bathes in comfort lacking any chance to reach the limit of their abilities. To guard against every adversity is to hide from existence and prevent the development of coping mechanisms and perseverance in the face of stress. We can gain dominant strength and greater clarity to push our limitations or we can surrender to our flawed nature and languish in mediocrity.

We must renew our humanity and recognize the importance of increasing legitimate direct human interactions. Disliking or hating people is not a sufficient justification to seek the destruction of people's lives, and such pettiness reeks of submission to the lower brain. Negative behavior willfully chosen is not only harmful to targets but to the mind of the aggressor, and eventually a person faces the responsibility of their own choices because the environment and biology can only be influencers. A rational human must ultimately determine what truly is more important, shall they choose respectful coexistence that leads to societal progress or embrace aggression and violence as the semiconscious slave of fear and disgust.

GLOSSARY

Aggression: Hostile, intimidating, or combative behavior often related to frustration or irrational motivations.

Barbarity: The repeated inhumanity, cruelty, and brutal conduct used by human beings when they feel justified undertaking expansive acts of violence.

Capitalism: A system that relies on reciprocal barter trade principles in market economies which allows participants the opportunity for social and financial advancement but does not provide assurances of success. Such economies require strong regulation to impede corruption and the manipulation of related economic systems.

Cheka: The Bolshevik secret police created by Vladimir Lenin to identify and neutralize counter-revolutionary movements and members.

CIA: The Central Intelligence Agency is the most famous and, in some circles, most distrusted intelligence organization in the United States.

Clandestine: Concealment and illicit means that are used to protect secret undertakings.

Cute Aggression: The human brain's jarring defense that floods a person's mind with unpleasant or violent thoughts to counteract overwhelming feelings of adoration it perceives as dangerous.

Defector: A defector is a person who betrays their side in a conflict for opposing forces to the detriment of their original side. **Often,** they are a citizen whose public disloyalty potentially is utilized to advance hostile external intelligence goals.

Disgust: One of the human brain's neurobiological features that judges competing sources of possible offensive, unsanitary, and animalistic behavior that may incite a person to confrontation, retreat, or paralyzing inaction.

Fear: One of the human brain's neurobiological features that judges competing sources of possible and proven danger that may incite a person to confrontation, retreat, or paralyzing inaction.

FBI: The Federal Bureau of Investigation is among the most powerful and longest existing American intelligence groups.

FSB: The Russian Federal Security Service that was created from the remnants of the KGB.

GRU: The Red Army's General Staff Chief Directorate that served as the primary military intelligence group during the Soviet era.

KGB: The Soviet State Security Commission is among the most feared Cold War Soviet intelligence groups known for its expansive programs targeting defectors and responding to several public betrayals with assassination.

NKGB: The People's Commissariat for State Security, a KGB predecessor group emerging from the NKVD that existed during the nineteen forties and fifties under the control of Lavrentiy Beria.

NKVD: The Soviet People's Commissariat for Internal Affairs membership served the Interior Ministry as secret police and developed toxins for use in assassinations.

The Office of Strategic Services: This WWII era United States intelligence and paramilitary group is among the founding official collaborations to establish modern American clandestine operations. Some of the most successful and controversial practices utilized by the OSS were adopted for later military and civilian organizations to varying results.

Pressure: Regular performance challenges in any competitive field that require coping skills to overcome.

SIS (MI6): A division of the British Secret Intelligence Service that is responsible for conducting foreign operations.

Socialism: An economic system desiring more equally distributed resources that counts upon its political leadership to control prices, wages, and production. Such economies have often used punitive measures to enact their policy and thus require strong public opposition to violence and constant refinement to prevent tyrannical regimes.

Social Media: A digital means of communication that has positive and negative effects on users causing variations to human socialization that have not been completely determined because of the short amount of time social media has existed.

Slavery: The barbaric practice of human servitude that many nations and some religions propagated that can follow conquest. This practice and its later institutional versions were empowered by the economic profiteering of many nations across the planet.

Stress: Negative biological responses to undergoing increased levels of physical or mental tension.

SVR: The post-Soviet Foreign Intelligence Service of the Russian Federation crafted from policies developed by secret police groups such as the Checka and the KGB.

Tribalism: Significant loyalty to a group doctrine that can be held despite opposing facts.

Violence: The use of physical force intended to damage, harm, or destroy.

QUOTATIONS

CHAPTER 1: John C. Maxwell, Thinking for a Change: 11 Ways Highly Successful People Approach Life and Work, Hachette Book Group, 2003

CHAPTER 2: Claudia Dreifus, April 3, 2007, Finding Hope in Knowing the Universal Capacity for Evil, The New York Times, nytimes.com

CHAPTER 3: Paul J. Springer, "9/11 and the War on Terror: A Documentary and Reference Guide", Greenwood, 2016, p. 307

CHAPTER 4: Putin talks poison on Russian state TV as concerns grow over ill double agent, (August 3, 2018), Euronews, euronews.com

CHAPTER 5: Arthur Conan Doyle, (February, 1892), The Adventure of the Speckled Band, The Strand Magazine Issue 2, Stanford University, sherlockholmes.stanford.edu

NOTES

CHAPTER 1: Domination, Aggression, and Violence

[i] Larry J. Siever, (September 27, 2014), Neurobiology of Aggression and Violence, National Center for Biotechnology Information, United States Library of Medicine, National Institutes of Health, ncbi.nlm.nih.gov

[ii] R. Douglas Fields, (October 2, 2016), Humans Are Genetically Predisposed to Kill Each Other..., Psychology Today, psychologytoday.com

[iii] Henry R. Hermann, (2017), Dominance and Aggression in Human and Other Animals, Defining Dominance and Aggression, pp. 1-25

[iv] Ian Johnston, (September 28, 2016), Human evolved to have an instinct for deadly violence, researchers find..., The Independent, independent.co.uk

[v] R. Douglas Fields, (April 27, 2016), The Science of Violence, Psychology Today, psychologytoday.com

[vi] Ed Yong, (September 28, 2016), Humans: Unusually Murderous Mammals, Typically Murderous Primates, The Atlantic, theatlantic.com

[vii] Nicola Davis, (September 28, 2016), Natural born killer: humans predisposed to murder, study suggests, The Guardian, theguardian.com

[viii] Nicholas Wade, (September 17, 2002), Scientist At Work/Steven Pinker; In Nature vs. Nurture, a Voice for Nature, New York Times, nytimes.com

[ix] Hannah Holmes, The Well-Dressed Ape: A Natural History of Myself, Lyons Press, 2008, pp. 7-8

[x] Amina Khan, (March 29, 2017), Biology explains why men kill big game like Cecil the lion--and how that behavior might be stopped, Los Angeles Times, latimes.com

[xi] Mary K. Hart, Andrew W. Kratter, Philip H. Crowley, (January 1, 2016), Partner fidelity and reciprocal investments in the mating system of s simultaneous hermaphrodite, Behavioral Ecology Volume 27, Issue 5, pp. 1471-1479

[xii] Matthew H. McIntyre, Carolyn P. Edwards, (October, 2009), The Early Development of Gender Differences, University of Nebraska - Lincoln, digitalcommons.unl.edu, pp. 84-86

[xiii] Klaus A Mczek, Allan F. Mirsky, Gregory Carey, Joseph DeBold, and Adrian Raine, (1994), Understanding and Preventing Violence, Volume 2: Biobehavioral Influences, National Academy Press, nap.edu

[xiv] Glenn Weisfeld and Donald M Aytch, (Spring 1996), Biological Factors in Family Violence, Michigan Family Review Volume 2, Issue 1, pp. 25-39, quod.lib.umich.edu

[xv] Akko P. Kalma, Lieuwe Visser, Allerd Peeters, (Spring 1993), Sociable and aggressive dominance: Personality difference in leadership style?, The Leadership Quarterly, pp. 45-64

[xvi] The Early Development of Gender, p. 87-88

[xvii] Kate Fogarty and Garret D. Evans, (December 1999), The Hidden Benefits of Being an Involved Father, University of Florida, cfuf.org

[xviii] Ross Mackay, (March 2005), The Impact of Family Structure and Family change on Child Outcomes: A Personal Reading of the Research Literature, Social Policy Journal of New Zealand, pp. 112-113

[xix] Bret Stetka, (September 19 2017), Extended Adolescence: When 25 Is the New 18, Scientific American, scientificamerican.com

[xx] H. Holmes, The Well-Dressed Ape, pp. 126-127

[xxi] Thomas Elbert, Brigette Rockstroh, Iris Kolassa, Maggie Schauer, Frank Neuner, (2007), The Influence of Organized Violence and Terror on Brain and Mind- a Co-Constructive Perspective, pp. 1-5,6,7,8, 10

[xxii] Ibid

CHAPTER 2: Anti-Social Creatures

[xxiii] James Gorman, (January 23, 2012), Survival Ick Factor, New York Times, nytimes.com

[xxiv] Sofie Kent, Tracey J. Devonport, Andrew M. Lane, Andrew P. Friesen, (March 17, 2018), The Effects of Coping Interventions on Ability to Perform Under Pressure, Journal of Sports, Science, and Medicine, US Library of Medicine, ncbi.nlm.nih.gov

[xxv] John Hamilton, (December 31, 2018), When too cute is too much, the brain can get aggressive, National Public Radio, npr.org

[xxvi] Christopher Wanjek, (March 26, 2016), Rage Disorder Linked with Parasite Found in Cat Feces, Scientific American, scientificamerican.com

[xxvii] "The Biology of Humans at Our Best and Worst", Robert Sapolsky, Science and Frontiers of the Mind Initiative, Stanford University, October 24, 2017

[xxviii] Emily S. Rueb, (April 24, 2019), W.H.O. Says Limited on No Screen Time for Children Under 5, New York Times, nytimes.com

[xxix] Igor Pantic, (October 1, 2014), Online Social Networking and Mental Health, Cyberpsychology, Behavior, and Social Networking, pp. 652-657

[xxx] Menahem Krakowski and Karen Nolan, (February 28, 2017), Depressive Symptoms Associate With Aggression, Psychiatric Times Volume 34, Issue 2, psychiatrictimes.com

xxxi Christina Farr, (December 1, 2018), I quit Instagram and Facebook and it made me a lot happier- and that's a big problem for social media companies, CNBC News, cnbc.com

xxxii Catherine Price, (April 24, 2019), Putting Down Your Phone May Help You Live Longer, The New York Times, nytimes.com

xxxiii Soo Youn, (May 24, 2019), Crossfit quits Facebook and Instagram, citing privacy concerns, ABC News, abcnews.go.com

xxxiv Barret Wilson, (July 14, 2018), I Was the Mob Until the Mob Came for Me, Quillette, quillette.com

xxxv Cody Goodwin and Dave Lee, (May 13, 2019), When misinformation online leads to death threats, BBC, bbc.com

xxxvi Kate Kelland, (March 13, 2019), Online activists are silencing us, scientists say, Reuters, reuters.com

xxxvii Nicholas Wade, Scientist At Work/Steven Pinker; nytimes.com

xxxviii Shamard Charles, (March 14, 2019), Social media linked to rise in mental health disorders in teen, survey finds, NBC News, nbcnews.com

xxxix Natalie Wolochover, (July 25, 2012), Why Is Everyone on the Internet So Angry?, Scientific American, scientificamerican.com

xl Diane Bartz, (April 9, 2019), US senator introduce social media bill to ban 'dark patterns' tricks, Reuters, reuters.com

xli Chunka Mui, (October 15, 2018), Have You Committed A Facecrime Today?, Forbes Magazine, forbes.com

xlii Chris Frith, (December 2009), Role of facial expressions in social interactions, US Library of Medicine, ncbi.nlm.nih.gov

xliii David Brooks, (January 21, 2019), How We Destroy Lives Today, New York Times, nytimes.com xliv Kevin Roose, (March 15, 2019), A Mass Murder **of,** and for, the Internet, New York Times, nytimes.com

xlv Carl Miller, (March 9, 2019), It's ridiculously easy to manipulate Facebook with anger, Wired, wired.co.uk

xlvi Josh Gabbatiss, (July 19, 2017), Nasty, Brutish, and Short: Are Humans DNA-Wired to Kill?, Scientific American, scientificamerican.com

xlvii Weisfeld and Aytch, Biological Factors in Family Violence

xlviii Orjan Falk, Marta Wallinius, Sebastian Lundstrom, Thomas Frisell, Henrik Anckarsater, Nora Kerekes, (October 21, 2013), Social Psychiatry and Psychiatric Epistemology, ncbi.nlm.nih.gov, pp. 559-571

xlix The Scientific American Book of the Brain, Seeking the Criminal Element, Lyons Press, 2001, pp. 210, 211

l Ibid 209, 210

li Cathy Young, (February 22, 2018), When wives beat their husbands, no one wants to believe it, Los Angeles Times, latimes.com

lii Book of the Brain, 2001, p. 209

liii Erin Fuchs, (February 17, 2013), Professor Conducted A Huge Study to Find Out Why People Kill, Business Insider, businessinsider.com

liv Leah Giarratano, (July 2, 2012), 'Madness without confusion', Sydney Morning Herald, smh.com.au

lv Casey N. Cep, (June 22, 2016), The Indispensable Guide to Early American Murder, The New Yorker, newyorker.com

lvi Patrick Sauer, (October 14, 2015), The Story of the First Mass Murder in U.S. History..., Smithsonian Magazine, smithsonianmag.com

lvii Barbara Bradley Hagerty, (June 29, 2010), A Neuroscientist Uncovers A Dark Secret, National Public Radio, npr.org [lviii] Jack Pemment, (April 5, 2013), What Would We Find Wrong in the Brain of a Serial Killer?, Psychology Today, psychologytoday.com

[lix] Chris Hedges, (July 6, 2003), "What Every Person Should Know About War", New York Times, nytimes.com

[lx] "Biology of Humans at Our Best and Worst", R. Sapolsky

[lxi] R. Douglas Fields, The Science of Violence

[lxii] Mark A. Mattaini, (2003), Understanding and Reducing Collective Violence, Behavior and Social Issues, 12, University of Illinois Chicago, journals.uic.edu

[lxiii] Joanna Bourke, "An Intimate History of Killing: Face to Face Killing in Twentieth-Century Warfare", **Basic** Books, 1999, pp. 2-5

Chapter 3: Notable American Violence

[lxiv] "The Biology of Humans at Our Best and Worst"

[lxv] Christina Snyder, "Slavery in Indian Country", Harvard University Press, 2010, p. 6

[lxvi] Jeffery Kluger, (April 10, 2015), Here's What Happened in the Brain When People Kill, Time Magazine, time.com

[lxvii] Katrina Trinko, (December 19, 2018), If you're using 'white privilege' to shut people up, maybe you're the problem, USA Today, usatoday.com

[lxviii] Brett Molina, (January 16, 2019), CNN analyst Areva Martin accused radio host David Webb of 'white privilege.' Webb is black, USA Today, usatoday.com

[lxix] Andrew G. Garber, (Spring, 2010), The Indian War, Trend & Tradition Magazine, history.org

[lxx] C. Snyder, "Slavery in Indian Country", p. 4,

lxxi Ibid, pp. 5, 6

lxxii Ibid, p. 7, 8

lxxiii Kat Eschner, (March 8, 2017), The Horrible Fate of John Casor, The First Black Man to be Declared Slave for Life in America, Smithsonian Magazine, smithsonian.com

lxxiv Africans in America, (n.d.), From Indentured Servitude to Racial Slavery, PBS, pbs.org

lxxv "The Atlantic slave trade: What too few textbooks told you", Anthony Hazard, Ted-Ed Project, ted.com, 2014

lxxvi Manifest Destiny and Indian Removal, (n.d.), Smithsonian American Art Museum and Renwick Gallery, americanexperience.si.edu

lxxvii Historical Statistics of the United States, Colonial Times to 1970, (September 1975), United States Census Bureau, census.gov

lxxviii C. Snyder, p. 7

lxxix History of Lynchings, National Association for the Advancement of Colored People, naacp.org

lxxx The Logic Behind the Destruction of Dresden, (February 13, 2009), Spiegel Online, spiegel.de

lxxxi C. Hedges, What Every Person Should Know About War

lxxxii United States Office of the Historian, Milestones: 1945-1952, The Chinese Revolution of 1949, US State Department, history.state.gov

lxxxiiilxxxiii Russell Jack Smith, The Unknown CIA: My Three Decades with the Agency, Pergamon-Brassey's International Defense Publishers Inc, pp. 82-83

lxxxiv Central Intelligence Agency, Blue bird/Artichoke Soft File Review - "Kelly" - Dimitrov, D.A., A.R. Cinquegrana, Office of General Counsel, United States National Archives and Records Administration (NARA),

October 7, 1977, archives.gov, NARA Identification Number: 104-10404-100094

[lxxxv] CIA, Restricted File on Dimitrov, Dimitur Adamov, NARA, September 15, 1977, archives.gov, 104-10435-10071

[lxxxvi] Central Intelligence Agency, Overthrow of Premier Mossadeq of Iran: November 1952-August 1953, George Washington University National Security Archive, nsarchive2.gwu.edu, March 1954

[lxxxvii] Central Intelligence Agency, Operation PBSUCCESS, "A Study of Assassination", GWU National Security Archive, nsarchive2.gwu.edu

[lxxxviii] Ibid

[lxxxix] Casey P. DeSormier, Cold War Agency: The United States and the Failure of the Diem Experiment, (March 2017), Naval Post Graduate School, my.nps.edu, pp. 42-44

[xc] Senate Select Committee to Study Governmental Operations with Respect to Intelligence Activities, Miscellaneous Records of the Church Committee, Lumumba, Patrice, Assassination, The Mary Ferrell Foundation, maryferrell.org, 1975

[xci] CIA, Assassinations, NARA, archives.gov, June 16, 1975, p. 3-4

[xcii] CIA, Unsanitized copy of Diem Report, NARA, archives.gov, May 31, 1967, pp. 5-7

[xciii] Seymour M. Hersh, GIs Call Viet Killings 'Point Blank Murder', Cleveland Plain Dealer, November 20, 1969, cleveland.com

[xciv] Jon Wiener, (March 16, 2018), A forgotten hero stopped the My Lai massacre 50 years ago today, Los Angeles Times, latimes.com

[xcv] Was My Lai just one of the many massacres in Vietnam War?, (August 28, 2013), BBC News, bbc.com

[xcvi] United States State Department, Ambassador's Cable from Rio De Janiero, GWU National Security Archive, nsrchive2.gwu.edu, March 27, 1964

[xcvii] CIA, Departure of Goulart from Porto Alegre for Montevideo, GWU National Security Archive, nsrchive2.gwu.edu, April 2, 1964

[xcviii] CIA, CIA Library Reading Room, Activities in Chile, September 18, 2000, Central Intelligence Agency, cia.gov

[xcix] Beverly C. Tomek, MOVE, Encyclopedia of Greater Philadelphia, Mid-Atlantic Regional Center for Humanities at Rutgers-Camden, philadelphiaencyclopedia.org

[c] David Von Drehle and R. Jefferey Smith, (January 27, 1993), U.S. Strikes for Plot to Kill Bush, Washington Post, washingtonpost.com

Chapter 4: Notable Russian Violence

[ci] Tal Axelrod, (September 4, 2018), Trump wanted to assassinate Assad after chemical attack: Woodward book, The Hill, thehill.com

[cii] Danny Bird, (September 5, 2018), How the Red Terror' Exposed the True Turmoil of Soviet Russia 100 years ago, Time Magazine, time.com

[ciii] Holodomor: Memories of Ukraine's silent massacre, (November 23, 2013), BBC News, bbc.com

[civ] Ta-Nehisi Coates, (January 3, 2014), Grappling With Holodomor, The Atlantic, theatlantic.com

[cv] Jordan Peterson, The Gulag Archipelago confirmed the horrors of the Soviet Union, The Australian, theaustrialian.com

[cvi] Anne Applebaum, Death of a Writer: How Alexander Solzihenitsyn's The Gulag Archipelago changed the world, Slate, slate.com

[cvii] Calder Walton, (March 13, 2018), Russia has a long history of eliminating 'enemies of the state', Washington Post, washintonpost.com

cviii Jackie Mansky, (October 10, 2017), The True Story of the Death of Stalin, Smithsonian Magazine, smithsonianmag.com

cix CIA, Oswald 201 File (201-289248), Volume 27, Soviet Use of Assassination and Kidnapping, February 20, 1964, pp. 1-6, 8-9, 10-14

cx CIA, Case of Yuriy Ivanovich Nosenko, Volume IV, Parts 7-9, The Mary Ferrell Foundation, maryferrell.org, National Archives and Records Administration Identification Number: p. 664

cxi CIA, Oswald 201 File, Vol. 27, SU of Assassination..., pp. 3-4

cxii Ibid, pp. 15

cxiii Ibid, pp. 15, 17, 18-21

cxiv Ibid, pp. 22-23

cxv Jason Fagone, (February 18, 2018), The Amazing Story of the Russian Defector Who Changed his Mind, The Washingtonian, washingtonian.com

cxvi David Holley, (April 18, 2003), Russian Lawmaker is Slain, Los Angeles Times, articles.latimes.com

cxvii Shaun Walker, (October 5, 2006), The murder that killed free media in Russia, The Guardian, theguardian.com

cxviii Anna Politkovskaya, (n.d.), Deaths by Type Worldwide since 1992, Committee to Protect Journalists, cpj.org

cxix Jeremy Wilson, (March 11, 2016), Here's a list of Putin critics who've ended up dead, Business Insider, businessinsider.com

cxx Vladimir Kara-Murza, (July 20, 2018), What's really behind Putin's obsession with the Magnitsky Act, The Washington Post, washingtonpost.org

cxxi 2008 Georgia Russia Conflict Fast Facts, (April 3, 2018), CNN, cnn.com [cxxii] Luke Harding, (January 19, 2009), Human rights lawyer murdered in Moscow, The Guardian, theguardian.com

[cxxiii] Philip P. Pan, (July 16, 2009), Human Rights Activist Natalya Estemirova Killed in Chechnya, Washington Post, washingtonpost.com

[cxxiv] Russian Activist Natalya Estemirova found dead, (July 15, 2009), The Telegraph, telegraph.co.uk

[cxxv] Alexander Smith and Yuliya Talmazan, (November 28, 2018), Russian 'creeping annexation' hits Ukraine in Sea of Azov, NBC News, nbcnews.com

Chapter 5: Defying Aggression and Violence

[cxxvi] Russia Opposition politician Boris Nemtsov shot dead, (February 28, 2015), BBC News, bbc.com

[cxxvii] Leonid Bershidsky, (March 23, 2017), Russian Defector's Murder Sends a Chilling Message, Bloomberg, bloomberg.com

[cxxviii] The Latest: UK calls Security Council talks on poison case, (September 5, 2018), Associated Press, apnews.com

[cxxix] Jeff Stein, (March 31, 2018), From Moscow with Murder: Is Russia Hunting Defectors in America?, Newsweek Magazine, newsweek.com

[cxxx] Cristina Maza, (December 19, 2018), Russia vs. Ukraine: More Russians want the Soviet Union and Communism back amid continued tensions, Newsweek, newsweek.com

[cxxxi] John Glaser, March 17, 2017, NATO Expansion Is Unwise. Saying So Isn't Treasonous., Cato Institute, cato.org

[cxxxii] Vladimir Kara-Murza, (January 25, 2018), The Kremlin deploys its new law against 'undesirables', Washington Post, washingtonpost.com

[cxxxiii] Sarah Rainsford, (March 4, 2019), Russia's Jehovah's Witnesses claim state tortured them, BBC News, bbc.com

cxxxiv Andrew Osborn, (February 21, 2019), Putin to U.S.: I'm ready for another Cuban Missile-style crisis if you want one, Reuters, reuters.com

cxxxv Maria Vasilyeva and Shamil Zhumatov, (March 10, 2019), Thousands of Russian protest against internet restrictions, Reuters, reuters.com

ABOUT THE AUTHOR

C.A.A. Savastano is an author, speaker, and Editor-in-Chief of the Neapolis Media Group whose historical research focuses on intelligence, government, international politics, and human behavior. He has studied thousands of legal documents, written over seventy historical research articles; consulted for multiple experts in his field presented new research of public value, and makes regular appearances in the media.

CAMPANIA PARTNERS PUBLISHING

Other Books from C.A.A. Savastano:

Two Princes And A King: A Concise Review of Three Political Assassinations, Neapolis Media Group, 2016.

Other Books from Campania Partners:

The War State: The Cold War Origins of the Military-Industrial Complex And The Power Elite, by Michael Swanson, Campania Partners, 2013.

Judyth Vary Baker: In Her Own Words, by Walt Brown, PhD, Campania Partners, 2019.

In Denial: Secrets War With Air Strikes And Tanks?, by Larry Hancock, Campania Partners, 2020.

Made in the USA
Columbia, SC
29 September 2023

23594354R00107